300 Easy Recipes For Quick and Tasty Meals Instant Pot Cookbook

Michael Elliott

Warning-Disclaimer

The purpose of this book is to educate and entertain. The author or publisher does not guarantee that anyone following the techniques, suggestions, tips, ideas, or strategies will become successful. The author and publisher shall have neither liability or responsibility to anyone with respect to any loss or damage caused, or alleged to be caused, directly or indirectly by the information contained in this book.

Table of Contents

Introduction

Instant Pot is a famous cooking pot to save your time because it helps you to instantly cook meal. This advanced electric cooker is a multifunctional programmable device for cooking. The latest IP-DUO series can do the work of seven appliances, such as:

1. Pressure cooker

2. Slow cooker

3. Porridge Maker or rice cooker

4. Sauté pan

5. Steamer

6. Serving/warming pot

7. Yogurt maker

Instant pot can do all above functions and enable you to cook your favorite food in a few minutes. Cooking in an instant pot allows you to make your food delicious. You can cook lentils, vegetables, meat, rice, stews, soup, frying items, hummus, puddings, curry and desserts in instant pot. With just one touch of button, you can cook lots of food items.

You can use instant pot as a yogurt maker and cook flavorful meals to retain minerals and vitamins in your food items. Cooking in instant pot will prove helpful to prepare in controlled and sealed environment. Aroma and nutrients stay in the ingredients instead of dispersing around in your house. It will protect original juices of fruits, meat and fish. You can cook food in the steam of pressure cook; hence, there is no need to put extra water in instant pot. Make sure to add sufficient water to fill instant pot with steam. The minerals and vitamins will not be leached or dissolved away in instant pot. The steam surrounds food and air will not oxidize your food in the presence of heat.

It is great to cool broccoli, asparagus, and other vegetables while retaining their phytochemicals and green colors. Bones and meat can be cooked to tender quickly in instant pot, and the pork ribs will be completely separate from meat to make the chewable and easily absorb minerals and calcium. Cook bean and whole grain meal under pressure for soft texture and better taste. For some people, it can be difficult to understand the functioning of the instant pot to cook meat, beans, and vegetable. This book has the best instant pot recipes related to desserts, soup, meat, vegetables and fish recipes.

Cooking in instant pot is equally beneficial for housewives and working women. If you want to serve healthy and delicious food to you family without increasing clutter around you, this cookbook and instant pot can be a right combination for you. If you have less time to prepare party food, just follow the recipes given in this book and prepare yummy food for the party. Your guests will become a fan of your culinary skills.

This cookbook can make it easy for you to prepare dinner, lunch, breakfast, and snacks. Each and every recipe has detailed instructions to bring perfection in your cooking. This book will prove really beneficial to save your time and cook food without clutter. You can cook food instantly without disturbing other activities of your day. If you want to make your life convenient, grab you copy now and explore the incredible powers of the instant pot.

Some of the feature recipes included in this book are:

Instant Pot Lava Chocolate, Egg and Cheese Casserole, Creamy Spinach Simmer, Peanut Slabs, Roasted Turkey, Spaghetti Squash Delight, Orzo with Potato and Carrots, Potato and Zucchini Curry, Black Lentil Tacos, Tuna Pasta Braise, Ground Beef Zucchini Zoodles, Chicken Broccoli Soups, Potato Cream Soup, Cauliflower and Potato Cobbler, Fenugreek and Beef Curry, Hot Shredded Pork, Crispy Crum Fish, Creamy Tuna with Vegetables, Roasted Egg Gravy, Banana and Strawberry Pudding, Salty Fried Peanuts, Slow Cooked Beef Turnips and much more.

You can make all these recipes with your instant pot at home easily and quickly to start your journey toward a healthier and more comfortable way of life.

I am sure you will enjoy trying all the recipes presented in this book and you will most definitely feel like a chef before your guests once you serve those delicious and healthy meals.

Grab your copy today and love the mighty power of your instant pot.

So now, let's get started

Instant Pot Breakfast Recipes

1. Instant Pot Zucchini Tortilla

(Time: 15 minutes \ Servings: 3)

Ingredients:

3 eggs

1 large zucchini

1 onion, chopped

½ teaspoon thyme, chopped

¼ teaspoon salt

¼ teaspoon white pepper

2 tablespoons olive oil

Directions:

Cut the zucchini into thin strips and place aside. Crack the eggs in a medium bowl and whisk with a fork for 1 minute. Add the zucchini strips, onion, thyme, salt, and pepper, mix well.

Add 3-4 cups of water into the instant pot and place a trivet or stand it in.

Now spray a medium sized baking dish with olive oil, transfer the eggs mixture into a pan and place into a trivet. Cover the pot with a lid and let it cook on manual mode for 10 minutes. Serve hot.

2. Instant Pot Peachy Oats Crumble

(Time: 35 minutes \ Servings: 3)

Ingredients:

2 cups oats

½ cup peach juice

1 peach, sliced

1 cup milk

¼ cup brown sugar

4 tablespoons maple syrup

1 pinch salt

1 cup sour cream

2 tablespoons butter, melted

Directions:

Combine the oats, milk, peach juice, maple syrup, sour cream, brown sugar, and salt in a bowl.

Brush the instant pot with butter. Transfer the oats mixture to the instant pot and cover with a lid.

Cook on slow cook mode for 35 minutes. Transfer to a serving dish and place the peach slices.

Drizzle some maple syrup on top. Serve and enjoy.

3. Cheesy Instant Pot Spinach Casserole

(Time: 25 minutes \ Servings: 4)

Ingredients:

1 cup spinach, chopped

½ lb. cheddar cheese

½ lb. mozzarella cheese

1 onion, chopped

4 eggs, whisked

l yellow bell pepper, chopped

¼ teaspoon salt

¼ teaspoon black pepper

2 tablespoons olive oil

Directions:

In a bowl add the eggs, spinach, mozzarella cheese, cheddar cheese, bell pepper, and onion, mix well. Season with salt and pepper. Grease the instant pot with olive oil.

Transfer the spinach mixture to the instant pot and cover with a lid.

Let it cook for 25 minutes on slow cook mode. Serve hot and enjoy.

4. Instant Pot Cranberry Oatmeal

(Time: 40 minutes \ Servings: 5)

Ingredients:

2 cups oats

2 cups milk

1 egg, whisked

1 cup cranberry sauce

½ cup brown sugar

2 tablespoons honey

½ teaspoon ginger powder

1 pinch salt

4 tablespoons butter, melted

2 tablespoons olive oil

Directions:

Grease the instant pot with olive oil.

Combine the oats, milk, egg, butter, cranberry sauce, honey, brown sugar, ginger powder, and salt in a bowl. Transfer to the greased instant pot and cover with a lid.

Let it cook on slow cook mode for 40 minutes. Serve and enjoy.

5. Sweet Potatoes and Peanuts Smash

(Time: 45 minutes \ Servings: 4)

Ingredients:

4 sweet potatoes, peeled, boiled

1 cup heavy milk

½ cup coconut milk

¼ cup coconut flakes

1 cup peanuts

2 eggs, whisked

1 teaspoon vanilla extracts

¼ teaspoon green cardamom powder

½ cup brown sugar

¼ cup all-purpose flour

1 pinch salt

4 tablespoons butter, melted

Directions:

Mash the sweet potatoes with a fork and combine with peanuts and coconut flakes.

In a separate bowl, combine the flour, brown sugar, salt, cardamom powder, eggs, milk, coconut milk, and vanilla extract, mix well.

Mix this mixture with the sweet potatoes and transfer to the instant pot. Let it cook on slow cook mode for 40 minutes. Serve and enjoy.

6. Instant Pot Dates Granola

(Time: 35 minutes \ Servings: 2)

Ingredients:

2 cups granola

1 cup dates, seeded, halved

1 cup milk

¼ cup peanuts

½ cup coconut milk

¼ cup coconut flakes

1 egg, whisked

¼ cup brown sugar

1 pinch salt

2 tablespoons butter, melted

Directions:

In a bowl add the dates with milk and mash with fork till smooth. Now add the brown sugar, granola, salt, butter, peanuts, and egg, mix to combine. Transfer to a greased instant pot and let it cook for 35 minutes on slow cook mode. Serve and enjoy.

7. Strawberry and Mango Crunch

(Time: 35 minutes \ Servings: 5)

Ingredients:

2 cups strawberries, sliced

2 cups mango, chunks

1 cup mango juice

1 package biscuits, crumbled

½ cup all-purpose flour

1 cup milk

1 egg, whisked

¼ cup caster sugar

4 tablespoons butter, melted

Directions:

In a bowl add all-purpose flour, biscuits, egg, sugar, mango juice, and milk, mix well. Spread into a greased baking dish and press with a spoon a little bit. Now drizzle butter, place the mango chunks and strawberry chunks on top.

Place a trivet into the instant pot and add 3-4 cups of water in it. Put a baking dish on a trivet and cover the pot with a lid. Cook on manual mode for 30 minutes.

8. Spinach and Tomato Cheesy Braise

(Time: 50 minutes \ Servings: 4)

Ingredients:

1 cup baby spinach, sliced

2 tomatoes, chopped

1 cup mushrooms, sliced

1 teaspoon ginger powder

1 teaspoon garlic paste

4 oz. parmesan cheese, shredded

½ lb. mozzarella cheese, shredded

1 egg, whisked

¼ pinch salt

¼ teaspoon thyme

¼ teaspoon black pepper

2 tablespoons butter, melted

Directions:

In the instant pot add the butter and sauté garlic for 30 seconds on sauté mode.

Now add the spinach, tomatoes, thyme, salt, black pepper, egg, ginger powder, and mushrooms, mix well. Add the parmesan cheese, mozzarella cheese and mix thoroughly.

Cover with a lid and cook on slow cook mode for 45 minutes. Serve hot and enjoy

9. Black Berry Oatmeal

(Time: 45 minutes \ Servings: 2)

Ingredients:

1 cup oats

1 cup black berries

1 cup cream milk

¼ cup caster sugar

4 tablespoons honey

2 tablespoons butter, melted

Directions:

Combine the oats, cream milk, sugar, and butter in a bowl. Transfer oats mixture to the instant pot and place the blackberries on top, cover with a lid. Let it cook on slow cook mode for 35 minutes.

Drizzle honey on top while serving. Serve and enjoy.

10. Instant Pot Lava Chocolate

(Time: 30 minutes \ Servings: 3)

Ingredients:

1 cup raw chocolate, crumbled

½ cup cocoa powder

½ cup all-purpose flour

1 cup cream milk

1 egg, whisked

¼ cup caster sugar

4 tablespoons butter, melted

1 cup cream, whipped

Directions:

In a bowl, add the all-purpose flour, egg, cocoa powder, chocolate, sugar, butter, and milk, beat with beater for 1-2 minutes.

Transfer this mixture into the instant pot and cook on pressure cook mode for 30 minutes. Now transfer to a serving dish and top with whipped cream. Sprinkle some chocolate flakes. Serve and enjoy.

11. Stir Fried Potato and Squash

(Time: 30 minutes \ Servings: 5)

Ingredients:

3 potatoes, peeled, sliced

1 onion, chopped

1 cup yellow squash

½ teaspoon cayenne pepper

2-3 garlic cloves, minced

¼ teaspoon salt

¼ teaspoon cumin powder

2 tablespoons butter

Directions:

Melt butter in the instant pot on sauté mod and fry onion for 1 minute. Add the garlic and fry for 30 seconds. Now add the potatoes and squash, fry for 10 minutes on low heat.

Season with salt, cayenne pepper, and cumin powder. Add 1-2 splashes of water and cook on low heat for 15 minutes. Serve hot and enjoy.

12. Spicy Instant Pot Potatoes

(Time: 15 minutes \ Servings: 3)

Ingredients:

4 potatoes, peeled, boiled, diced

1 cup yellow squash

½ teaspoon chili flakes

1 teaspoon garlic paste

¼ teaspoon salt

¼ teaspoon cumin powder

¼ teaspoon cinnamon powder

¼ teaspoon black pepper

¼ teaspoon thyme

2 tablespoons olive oil

Directions:

Heat oil in instant pot on sauté mode and fry garlic for 30 seconds. Now add the potatoes and fry for 10 minutes. Add salt, chili flakes, thyme, cumin powder, and cumin powder.

Transfer to a serving platter and serve. Enjoy.

13. Instant Pot Creamy Spinach Simmer

(Time: 25 minutes \ Servings: 4)

Ingredients:

2 cups baby spinach, chopped

1 cup heavy cream

½ cup coconut milk

¼ teaspoon white pepper

½ cup cheddar cheese

¼ teaspoon salt

2 tablespoons caster sugar

2 tablespoons olive oil

Directions:

Add spinach to the instant pot and mix with oil, milk, cream, cheese, sugar, salt, and pepper.

Cover with a lid and cook on pressure cook mode for 15 minutes.

Transfer to a serving dish and serve. Enjoy

14. Instant Pot Bowl Egg

(Time: 15 minutes \ Servings: 1)

Ingredients:

1 egg

1 bun, cut from top

1 pinch salt

¼ teaspoon dill, chopped

1 tablespoon red bell pepper, chopped

2 tablespoons olive oil

Directions:

Brush the bin with oil and crack the egg inside it. Sprinkle salt, dill and red bell pepper.

Transfer to the instant pot and cook on pressure cook more for 10 minutes. Now transfer to a serving dish and top with cap of bun.

Enjoy.

15. Egg and Chicken Casserole

(Time: 30 minutes \ Servings: 4)

Ingredients:

3 oz. chicken breast, cut into small pieces

3 eggs, whisked

1 onion, chopped

3-4 garlic cloves, minced

½ lb. mozzarella cheese, shredded

2 oz. parmesan cheese

¼ teaspoon salt

¼ teaspoon black pepper

¼ teaspoon thyme

2 tablespoons butter

Directions:

Melt butter in the instant pot on sauté mod and fry onion with garlic for 1-2 minutes. Now add the chicken and fry until golden brown. Add salt, black pepper, thyme, and mix well.

Now add egg, parmesan cheese, mozzarella cheese and mix thoroughly. Cover with a lid on and cook on pressure cook mode for 20 minutes. Transfer to a serving platter, serve and enjoy.

16. Potatoes and Ground Egg

(Time: 25 minutes \ Servings: 3)

Ingredients:

2 potatoes, peeled, chopped

3 eggs, whisked

½ teaspoon chili powder

¼ teaspoon salt

¼ teaspoon cumin powder

¼ teaspoon cinnamon powder

¼ teaspoon black pepper

3 tablespoons olive oil

Directions:

Heat 2 tablespoons of oil on sauté mode and transfer the eggs mixture, let it cook for 1 minute then flip side it and cook it for another minute. Now transfer the eggs to a platter and let it cool.

Crumble the eggs with a fork. Now add the remaining oil and fry the potatoes for 4-5 minutes or until softened. Season with salt, chili powder, black pepper, cumin powder, and cumin powder.

Transfer the crumbled eggs and stir well. Put to a serving dish and serve hot. Enjoy.

17. Creamy Instant Pot Egg Casserole

(Time: 15 minutes \ Servings: 3)

Ingredients:

4 eggs, whisked

1 onion, sliced

1 green chili, chopped

1 red bell pepper, chopped

½ lb. mozzarella cheese, shredded

¼ teaspoon salt

¼ teaspoon black pepper

¼ teaspoon dried basil

2 tablespoons butter

Directions:

Melt butter on sauté mode and sauté onion for 30 seconds. Now add the bell pepper, and fry for a minute. Transfer the eggs, mozzarella cheese, green chilies, and season with basil, salt and pepper.

Cover with a lid and cook on pressure cook mode for 10 minutes. Transfer to a serving dish and serve. Enjoy.

18. Cauliflower and Potato Cobbler

(Time: 25 minutes \ Servings: 3)

Ingredients:

3 potatoes, peeled, chopped

1 onion, chopped

1 cup cauliflower, chopped

¼ teaspoon garlic paste

½ teaspoon black pepper

¼ teaspoon salt

¼ teaspoon cumin powder

2 tablespoons olive oil

Directions:

Heat oil on sauté mode and sauté onion for 1 minute. Now add the potatoes and cook until golden.

Season with salt, black pepper, and cumin powder. Transfer the cauliflower and mix well.

Let it cook for 5 minutes and stir continuously. Put to a serving dish and serve hot. Enjoy.

19. Instant Pot Hot Scrambled Egg

(Time: 15 minutes \ Servings: 2)

Ingredients:

4 eggs, whisked

¼ teaspoon salt

1 cup chicken broth

¼ teaspoon black pepper

¼ teaspoon dill, chopped

2 tablespoons olive oil

Directions:

Heat oil in the instant pot on sauté mode and pour whisked eggs, crumble the eggs with a fork continuously and add the chicken broth. Now season with salt and pepper.

When chicken broth is dried out transfer the egg scramble to a serving dish and top with dill. Serve and enjoy.

20. Sweet Potato Mayo Casserole with Cream

(Time: 25 minutes \ Servings: 2)

Ingredients:

2 sweet potatoes, peeled, sliced

1 cup mayonnaise

1 cup heavy cream

1 cup chicken broth

1 red onion, sliced

½ teaspoon chili powder

¼ teaspoon salt

2 tablespoons olive oil

Directions:

Heat oil in the instant pot on sauté mod and sauté onion for 1 minute. Now add the sweet potatoes and stir for 1-2 minutes.

Add the chicken broth, salt and let to cook on low heat for 20-25 minutes or until sweet potatoes become softened. Now stir in mayonnaise, and cream.

Transfer to a serving dish and sprinkle chili powder on top.

21. Traditional Chickpea Curry with Potatoes

(Time: 25 minutes \ Servings: 3)

Ingredients:

1 cup chickpea, boiled

1 onion, chopped

1 tomato, chopped

2 potatoes, boiled, peeled, sliced

¼ teaspoon salt

½ teaspoon chili powder

2 tablespoons olive oil

Directions:

Heat oil in the instant pot on sauté mod and sauté onion for 1 minute. Add the tomatoes and fry well.

Now add the chickpea and potatoes and stir for 1-2 minutes. Season with salt and pepper.

Cook for 5-10 minutes. Transfer to a serving dish and sprinkle chili powder on top.

22. Mango Pudding

(Time: 25 minutes \ Servings: 2)

Ingredients:

1 cup mango, chunks

1 cup orange juice

1 pear, chopped

1 apple, chopped

1 cup milk

Directions:

In the instant pot add all ingredients and stir to combine.

Let it cook on slow cook mode for 50 minutes.

Serve and enjoy.

23. Instant Pot Brown Sugar and Carrot Shake

(Time: 25 minutes \ Servings: 2)

Ingredients:

4 carrots, peeled, sliced

2 cups milk

1 cup mango juice

½ cup brown sugar

1 cup whipped cream

Directions:

In the instant pot add all ingredients and cover with a lid. Let it cook for 50 minutes on slow cook mode. Transfer to a blender and blend until puree.

Place into a serving dish and top with whipped cream. Serve and enjoy

24. Instant Pot Oatmeal Pancakes

(Time: 25 minutes \ Servings: 4)

Ingredients:

1 cup oats

1 cup all-purpose flour

½ cup caster sugar

¼ teaspoon baking soda

½ teaspoon baking powder

2 eggs

1 cup heavy milk

2 tablespoons sour cream

4 tablespoons honey

1 pinch salt

4 tablespoons butter

Few strawberries, for garnishing

Directions:

Sift flour, sugar, baking powder, baking soda, salt and place aside.

Now beat the eggs for a minute and add in milk, sour cream and mix well.

Add the sifted flour mixture and oats, mix thoroughly with a spatula.

Melt butter in the instant pot.

Ladle the butter in the pot and spread in the form of cake. Let it cook for 2-3 minutes from 1 side, then flip side and let to cook till nicely brown. Transfer to a serving platter and drizzle honey.

Top with strawberries and enjoy.

25. Peanut Slabs

(Time: 45 minutes \ Servings: 4)

Ingredients:

1 cup peanuts, roughly chopped

1 cup all-purpose flour

¼ cup caster sugar

¼ cup butter

1 cup strawberry jam

¼ cup almonds, sliced

½ teaspoon baking powder

¼ teaspoon salt

Directions:

In a bowl, add flour, sugar, baking powder, salt, almonds, peanuts, and mix well.

Beat butter until fluffy and add in flour mixture; stir.

Now take a greased baking dish and spread half of the flour mixture at bottom and press very well with the back of spoon.

Spread strawberry jam evenly.

Now transfer remaining flour mixture at to and spread all over, press with spoon lightly.

Place a trivet in the instant pot and transfer the dish on it.

Let it cook on pressure cook mode for 35 minutes.

26. Instant Pot Lentils with Tomato and Cucumber

(Time: 25 minutes \ Servings: 2)

Ingredients:

1 cup lentils, soaked

2 tomatoes, chopped

1 cucumber, chopped

1 onion, chopped

1 teaspoon ginger paste

1 teaspoon garlic paste

1 bay leaf

¼ teaspoon salt

3 cups chicken broth

¼ teaspoon black pepper

2 tablespoons olive oil

Directions:

Heat oil in the instant pot on sauté mod and fry onion with ginger garlic paste and bay leaf for 1 minute. Add lentils and fry for 4-5 minutes. Add the chicken broth, salt, black pepper, and let to cook on pressure cook mode for 20 minutes.

Now add the tomatoes and cucumber, let it cook for 5 minutes. Transfer to a serving dish and serve hot. Enjoy

27. Spinach Frittata

(Time: 35 minutes \ Servings: 3)

Ingredients:

1 cup gram flour

1 cup spinach, chopped

¼ teaspoon chili flakes

¼ cup mushrooms, sliced

½ teaspoon salt

1 cup cooking oil

Directions:

In a bowl, add the gram flour, mushrooms, spinach, salt, chili flakes and mix well.

Add ¼ cup water and make a thick batter. Heat oil in the instant pot and drop a spoon full of butter into oil. Fry until golden brown. Serve with cilantro sauce and enjoy

28. Lemony Chicken Pasta

(Time: 35 minutes \ Servings: 3)

Ingredients:

1 package pasta, boiled

¼ lb. chicken, breasts

4 tablespoons lemon juice

½ cup tomato ketchup

2 tablespoons olive oil

Directions:

Heat oil in the instant pot and add the chicken, fry until golden brown. Add the pasta and fry for 1-2 minutes. Now add ketchup and mix well. Let it cook on medium heat for 1-2 minutes.

Turn off the heat and transfer to a serving dish. Drizzle lemon juice and serve.

29. Lamb with Thyme

(Time: 55 minutes \ Servings: 4)

Ingredients:

½ lb. lamb, pieces

2 carrots, sliced

3 tablespoons thyme springs

1 teaspoons salt

3 cups water

Directions:

In the instant pot add the lamb pieces, carrots, thyme, salt and water. Cover and cook on pressure cook mode for 50-55 minutes. Serve with boiled rice or bread.

30. White Beans and Broccoli Curry

(Time: 35 minutes \ Servings: 4)

Ingredients:

1 cup white bean, boiled

1 cup broccoli, florets

½ teaspoon salt

3 tablespoons cooking oil

1 cup tomato sauce

3 cups chicken broth

Directions:

In the instant pot add beans, chicken broth, tomato sauce, broccoli florets, cooking oil and salt.

Let it cook on low heat for 30-35 minutes on pressure cook mode. Transfer into serving bowls.

31. Instant Pot Chickpea Curry

(Time: 35 minutes \ Servings: 4)

Ingredients:

2 cups, chickpeas, boiled

2 tomatoes, chopped

¼ cup tomato puree

2 medium onion, chopped

1 teaspoon cumin seeds

1 teaspoon garlic paste

¼ teaspoon turmeric powder

¼ teaspoon salt

1 cup vegetable broth

¼ teaspoon chili powder

¼ teaspoon dry coriander powder

½ teaspoon cinnamon powder

2 tablespoons olive oil

Directions:

Heat oil in the instant pot on sauté mode and add cumin seeds, let it pop. Now add onion and fry until lightly golden.

Add in garlic, tomatoes, tomato puree, salt, chili powder, turmeric powder and fry for 4-5 minutes.

Now add the chickpea and stir for 1-2 minutes. Transfer the vegetable broth, cover with a lid and cook on manual mode for 30 minutes.

Sprinkle coriander powder and cinnamon powder, mix and put to a serving dish. Serve with rice and enjoy.

32. Instant Pot Chickpea Salad

(Time: 25 minutes \ Servings: 3)

Ingredients:

1 cups, chickpeas, soaked

1 carrot, sliced

1 cup mango chunks

½ cup pineapple chunks

1 cucumber, sliced

¼ teaspoon salt

2 tablespoons vinegar

1 tablespoon olive oil

4 cups water

Directions:

In the instant pot add water and chickpeas, cover with a lid and let it boil on pressure cook mode for 30 minutes.

Now throw the water and add the cucumber, pineapples, mangoes, carrots, salt, pineapple juice, vinegar, and olive oil, let to cook for 5 minutes on pressure cook mode. Transfer the salad to a serving bowl, serve and enjoy.

33. Instant Pot Roasted Turkey

(Time: 50 minutes \ Servings: 4)

Ingredients:

1 while turkey

1 teaspoon garlic paste

¼ teaspoon salt

¼ teaspoon chili powder

½ teaspoon black pepper

¼ teaspoon thyme

¼ teaspoon rosemary

½ teaspoon cinnamon powder

3 tablespoons lemon juice

4 tablespoons orange juice

3 tablespoons olive oil

Directions:

In a bowl combine orange juice, lemon juice, thyme, rosemary, garlic paste salt, pepper, chili powder, olive oil, and cinnamon powder, mix well. Pour onto the turkey and rub with hands all over.

Transfer the turkey in a greased instant pot and cover with a lid. Cook on pressure cook mode for 45-50 minutes. Serve and enjoy.

34. Instant Pot Creamy Broccoli Stew

(Time: 45 minutes \ Servings: 4)

Ingredients:

1 cup heavy cream	¼ teaspoon turmeric powder
4 oz. parmesan cheese	¼ teaspoon salt
1 cup broccoli florets	¼ teaspoon black pepper
2 carrots, sliced	½ cup vegetable broth
½ teaspoon garlic paste	4 tablespoon butter

Directions:

Melt butter in the instant pot on sauté mode. Now add garlic, sauté for 30 seconds. Now add broccoli and carrots, cook until softened. Stir in the vegetable broth and cover with a lid.

Cook on slow cook mode for 40 minutes. Serve and enjoy.

35. Cellini Beans with Baby Broccoli and Carrots

(Time: 55 minutes \ Servings: 5)

Ingredients:

2 cup Cellini beans, soaked	½ teaspoon white pepper
2 carrots, sliced	2 tablespoons lemon juice
1 cup broccoli florets	3 cups chicken broth
¼ teaspoon salt	3 tablespoons olive oil

Directions:

In the instant pot, add the Cellini beans, carrots, broccoli, salt, pepper, lemon juice, chicken broth, and olive oil, stir and cover with a lid. Cook on pressure cook mode for 50-55 minutes. Serve and enjoy.

36. Instant Pot Cheesy Mac

(Time: 60 minutes \ Servings: 3)

Ingredients:

1 package macaroni

6 oz. mozzarella cheese

¼ cup cream cheese

1 cup parmesan cheese

2-3 garlic cloves

¼ teaspoon black pepper

¼ teaspoon salt

½ cup vegetable broth

2 tablespoons butter

Directions:

Set the instant pot on sauté mode and melt butter. Sauté garlic for 30 seconds and add vegetable broth. Add in the the macaroni, mozzarella cheese, parmesan cheese, and cream cheese.

Season with salt and pepper. Cover the pot with a lid and let it cook on slow cook mode for 60 minutes. Serve and enjoy.

37. Instant Pot Broccoli Pasta

(Time: 35 minutes \ Servings: 3)

Ingredients:

1 package pasta

1 cup broccoli florets

1 teaspoon garlic paste

¼ teaspoon salt

1 cup vegetable broth

¼ teaspoon white pepper

2 cups chicken broth

2 tablespoons lemon juice

2 tablespoons olive oil

Directions:

In the instant pot, add garlic and oil and sauté for 1 minute on sauté mode. Add broccoli and stir well. Pour in the chicken broth with the pasta and mix well. Season with salt and pepper.

Cover with a lid and cook on manual mode for 30 minutes. Serve with rice and enjoy.

38. Instant Pot Spicy Chickpea Stew

(Time: 35 minutes \ Servings: 4)

Ingredients:

2 cups, chickpeas, boiled
3 tomatoes, chopped
3 small onions, chopped
1 teaspoon garlic paste
¼ teaspoon ginger paste
¼ teaspoon turmeric powder
¼ teaspoon salt

¼ teaspoon chili powder
¼ teaspoon cayenne pepper
¼ teaspoon cinnamon powder
½ teaspoon cumin powder
3 cups chicken broth
2 tablespoons olive oil

Directions:

Heat oil in the instant pot on sauté mode; add onion and fry until transparent.

Add in garlic, ginger, tomatoes, salt, cayenne pepper, chili powder, turmeric powder and fry for 4-5 minutes. Now add the chickpea and stir fry for 5 minutes. Transfer the chicken broth, cover with a lid and cook on manual mode for 30 minutes. Sprinkle cumin powder and cinnamon powder.

Transfer to a serving dish and serve.

39. Spaghetti Squash Delight

(Time: 35 minutes \ Servings: 3)

Ingredients:

1 squash, halved
3 tomatoes, chopped
1 onion, sliced
2-3 garlic cloves, minced
4 cups water

1 teaspoon basil, chopped
¼ teaspoon sea salt
2 tablespoons caster sugar
5 tablespoons butter

Directions:

In the instant pot add water and place a trivet in the pot. Transfer squash on trivet and cover the pot with a lid. Let it cook on pressure cook mode for 25 minutes. When squash is softened remove from the pot and transfer to a platter. Shred with fork.

Now melt butter in the instant pot on sauté mode and sauté onion with garlic for 1 minute. Stir in shredded squash and fry for 2-3 minutes. Season with salt and sugar, mix thoroughly.

Put to a serving platter and sprinkle basil on top. Serve hot and enjoy.

40. Hot Red Beans Curry

(Time: 60 minutes \ Servings: 5)

Ingredients:

1 cup red beans, soaked overnight

2 tomatoes, chopped

1 medium onion, chopped

1 teaspoon garlic paste

¼ teaspoon turmeric powder

¼ teaspoon salt

¼ teaspoon chili powder

¼ teaspoon cinnamon powder

½ teaspoon cumin powder

2 cups chicken broth

2 cups water

1 green chili

2 tablespoons olive oil

Directions:

Add water and red beans in instant pot and let it boil for 30 minutes on pressure cook mode. Now drain out the water and drain out the beans; place aside.

Heat oil in the instant pot on sauté mode and add onion and fry until transparent. Add garlic, tomatoes, salt, chili powder, turmeric powder and fry for 5 minutes. Now add the red beans and stir fry for 5 minutes.

Stir in the chicken broth and green chili, cover with a lid and cook on manual mode for 20 minutes.

Sprinkle cumin powder and cinnamon powder.

Transfer to a serving dish and serve.

41. Black Lentils in Instant Pot

(Time: 45 minutes \ Servings: 5)

Ingredients:

1 cup black lentils, soaked overnight

2 tomatoes, chopped

1 teaspoon garlic paste

¼ teaspoon ginger paste

¼ teaspoon turmeric powder

¼ teaspoon salt

¼ teaspoon chili powder

2 cups chicken broth

2 cups water

2 tablespoons olive oil

1 avocado, for garnishing

Directions:

Add water, lentils, turmeric powder, and chili powder and let it boil for 30 minutes on pressure cook mode. Now transfer the lentils with the stew in a bowl and place aside.

Heat oil in the instant pot on sauté mod and add garlic with ginger, and fry for 30 seconds. Add tomatoes, salt, and fry for 5-6 minutes. Stir in the lentils and chicken broth, cover with a lid.

Cook on manual mode for 15 minutes. Transfer to a serving dish and top with avocado slices. Serve.

42. Tropic Ginger Zest Red Lentils

(Time: 55 minutes \ Servings: 6)

Ingredients:

1 ½ cup red lentils, soaked overnight

2 tomatoes, chopped

¼ teaspoon ginger paste

¼ teaspoon turmeric powder

¼ teaspoon salt

¼ teaspoon chili powder

2 cups chicken broth

1 cup water

2 tablespoons olive oil

½ bunch fresh coriander, chopped, for garnishing

Directions:

Heat oil in the instant pot on sauté mod and add ginger, and fry for 30 seconds. Add tomatoes, salt, turmeric powder, chili powder, and fry for 5-6 minutes. Stir in lentils and fry for 5-10 minutes.

Stir in chicken broth and cover the pot with a lid. Cook on slow cook mode for 45 minutes. Transfer to a serving dish and sprinkle coriander. Serve.

43. Feta and Rice Stuffed Bell Peppers
(Time: 35 minutes \ Servings: 3)

Ingredients:

1 green bell pepper

1 red bell pepper

1 yellow bell pepper

½ cup rice, boiled

1 cup feta cheese

1 onion, sliced

1 teaspoon salt

2 tomatoes, chopped

1 teaspoon black pepper

2-3 garlic clove, minced

3 tablespoon lemon juice

3-4 green olives, chopped

3-4 tablespoons olive oil

Directions:

Grease the instant pot with olive oil. Make a cut at the top of bell peppers near stem. Take a bowl and add feta cheese, onion, olive, tomatoes, rice, salt, black pepper, garlic powder, lemon juice, and combine well. Fill up bell peppers with feta mixture and place inside the instant pot. Adjust the pot on slow cook mode. Serve and enjoy.

44. Orzo with Potatoes and Carrots
(Time: 45 minutes \ Servings: 3)

Ingredients:

1 cup white orzo

4 oz. parmesan cheese, shredded

2 carrots, sliced

2 potatoes, thinly sliced

1 onion, chopped

¼ teaspoon black pepper

½ teaspoon salt

2-3 garlic cloves, chopped

2 cups chicken broth

3 tablespoons cooking oil

Directions:

Set the instant pot on sauté mode. Heat oil and add onion with garlic, sauté until translucent.

Add potatoes, carrot, orzo, and chicken broth, mix well. Season with salt and pepper. Cover with a lid and let it prepare for 45 minutes on slow cook mode. Transfer to a serving dish and top with parmesan cheese. Serve and enjoy.

45. Spinach Orzo
(Time: 40 minutes \ Servings: 4)

Ingredients:

1 cup white orzo

1 cup baby spinach, chopped

1 cup cream cheese

¼ teaspoon black pepper

½ teaspoon salt

2-3 garlic cloves, chopped

2 cups vegetable broth

2 tablespoons cooking oil

Directions:

Set instant pot on sauté mode and heat oil. Sauté garlic for 30 seconds. Add orzo, spinach, salt and pepper and cook for 1-2 minutes. Now add chicken broth, stir well.

Cover with a lid and let it prepare for 35 minutes on slow cook mode. Now add cream cheese and cook for another 5 minutes on low heat. Serve and enjoy.

46. Chill Garlic Eggplant Pasta
(Time: 30 minutes \ Servings: 3)

Ingredients:

1 package pasta

1 large egg plant, sliced

1 cup chili garlic sauce

2 tablespoons barbecue sauce

½ cup tomato ketchup

¼ teaspoon chili powder

2-3 garlic cloves, chopped

2 cups vegetable broth

2 tablespoons cooking oil

Directions:

Set the instant pot on sauté mode and heat oil. Fry garlic for 30 seconds. Add eggplants and fry until nicely golden. Transfer the eggplant to a separate bowl and place aside.

Now in the instant pot add chili garlic sauce, tomato ketchup, chili powder, barbecue sauce, vegetable broth and stir well. Add pasta and mix, cover with a lid and let it prepare for 35 minutes on slow cook mode. Now add the eggplant and mix thoroughly. Serve and enjoy.

47. Cottage Cabbage Mac

(Time: 30 minutes \ Servings: 3)

Ingredients:

1 package macaroni	¼ teaspoon salt
1 cup cabbage, copped	¼ teaspoon white pepper
1 cup cottage cheese, shredded	2 cups vegetable broth
2-3 garlic cloves, chopped	2 tablespoons cooking oil

Directions:

Set the instant pot on sauté mode, heat oil and fry garlic for 30 seconds. Add cabbage and fry for 1-2 minutes. Now add vegetable broth, macaronic, salt, pepper, cheese and cove up with a lid.

Let it prepare for 35 minutes on slow cook mode.

48. Slow Cooked Spiced Cabbage

(Time: 60 minutes \ Servings: 2)

Ingredients:

1 cabbage, halved	1 tablespoons soya sauce
¼ teaspoon salt	1 teaspoon garlic powder
½ teaspoon thyme	2 tablespoons olive oil
¼ teaspoon black pepper	

Directions:

In a bowl combine soya sauce, salt, pepper, thyme, garlic powder, and olive oil. Place cabbage into a greased instant pot. Pour this mixer over cabbage.

Cove the pot and set to slow cook mode for 60 minutes. Serve and enjoy.

49. Cauliflower and Asparagus Pasta

(Time: 50 minutes \ Servings: 3)

Ingredients:

1 package pasta

½ cup peas

¼ cup cauliflower florets

1 cup asparagus, cut into 1 inch slices

1 cup basil pesto

¼ teaspoon black pepper

2-3 garlic cloves, chopped

2 cups vegetable broth

¼ teaspoon salt

2 tablespoons cooking oil

Directions:

Set the instant pot on sauté mode and heat oil. Fry garlic for 30 seconds. Add all vegetables fry for 4-5 minutes. Add pasta and vegetable broth and stir well. Season with salt, basil pesto, and pepper.

Let it cook on slow cooker mode for 50 minutes. Serve and enjoy.

50. Potato and Zucchini Curry

(Time: 40 minutes \ Servings: 3)

Ingredients:

2 potatoes, peeled, diced

2 zucchini, sliced

¼ teaspoon chili powder

½ cup tomato puree

1 teaspoon garlic powder

2 cups vegetable broth

¼ teaspoon salt

2 tablespoons cooking oil

Directions:

Set the instant pot on sauté mode and heat oil. Fry garlic for 30 seconds.

Transfer tomatoes, chili powder, salt and fry.

Add the potatoes with zucchini and fry for 10-15 minutes.

Then add the pasta and vegetable broth and stir well.

Let it cook on slow cooker mode for 20 minutes. Serve and enjoy.

51. Instant Pot Cauliflower Carrots Risotto

(Time: 65 minutes \ Servings: 4)

Ingredients:

1 cup cauliflower, florets

2 carrots, sliced

1 oz. tofu

1 onion, thinly sliced

1 teaspoon garlic paste

2 tomatoes, chopped

1 teaspoon black pepper

½ teaspoon salt

1 cup chicken broth

2 tablespoons cooking oil

Directions:

Set the instant pot on slow cook mode. Combine cauliflowers, carrots, tofu, tomatoes, onion, garlic paste, vegetable broth, and cooking oil. Season with salt and black pepper.

Cover and cook for 60 minutes on pressure cook mode. Serve and enjoy.

52. Chicken Orzo Soup

(Time: 45 minutes \ Servings: 3)

Ingredients:

1 cup orzo, boiled

1 cup chicken boneless, pieces

1 carrot, sliced

1 asparagus stem

½ cup spinach leaves

Black pepper and salt to taste

3 tablespoons cooking oil

3 cups chicken broth

Directions:

Heat oil in the instant pot and add chicken pieces, fry until lightly brown on sauté mode. Sprinkle salt and fry.

Now add orzo, spinach, carrots, asparagus, chicken broth, cover and leave to cook on low heat for 30-35 minutes on manual mode. Transfer into serving bowls, sprinkle black pepper on top. Enjoy.

53. Stir Fried Shrimps

(Time: 25 minutes \ Servings: 3)

Ingredients:

1 cup shrimps

4-5 garlic cloves, chopped

½ teaspoon salt

1 teaspoon black pepper

3 tablespoons olive oil

Directions:

Heat oil in the instant pot and add garlic cloves, sauté for 1 minute on sauté mode. Now add shrimps and fry until golden brown. Sprinkle salt and black pepper, mix thoroughly.

Turn off hat and transfer into a serving dish. Serve and enjoy.

54. Carrot and Broccoli Stew

(Time: 55 minutes \ Servings: 3)

Ingredients:

1 cup broccoli, florets

1 cup carrots, sliced

½ teaspoon salt

1 teaspoon black pepper, freshly ground

3 cups chicken broth

1 cup cream

Directions:

Add broccoli florets, cream, carrots, salt, chicken broth and toss well. Let it cook on low heat for 40-45 minutes on stew mode. Transfer into serving bowls and sprinkle black pepper on top.

Enjoy.

55. Creamy Pumpkin Puree Soup

(Time: 55 minutes \ Servings: 3)

Ingredients:

1 cup pumpkin puree

2 cup chicken broth

4-5 garlic cloves

Salt and black pepper to taste

1 cup cream

2 tablespoons olive oil

Directions:

In the instant pot add all ingredients and leave to cook on low heat for 40-45 minutes on stew mode.

After that transfer into a serving dish and food processor and blend well. Add to a serving bowl and serve.

56. Garlicky Roasted Potatoes

(Time: 45 minutes \ Servings: 3)

Ingredients:

3 large potatoes, cut into 1 inch slices

1 teaspoon garlic powder

1 teaspoon black pepper

1 teaspoons salt

4 tablespoons olive oil

Directions:

In a bowl add olive oil, garlic powder, salt, black pepper and mix.

Now add the potatoes and toss well.

Transfer into the instant pot and let it roast on pressure cook mode for 15-20 minutes.

Serve hot and enjoy.

57. Instant Pot Creamy Mushrooms

(Time: 25 minutes \ Servings: 3)

Ingredients:

1 cup mushrooms, sliced

1 cup cream

½ cup cream cheese

¼ teaspoon black pepper

½ teaspoon salt

2 garlic cloves, minced

2 tablespoons olive oil

Directions:

Set the instant pot on sauté mode, stir in garlic and fry for 1 minute. Add oil and sauté mushrooms for 4-5 minutes. Stir in cream, chicken broth, cream cheese and season with salt and pepper.

Let it prepare for 20-25 minutes on high pressure mode. Serve and enjoy.

58. Black Lentils Tacos

(Time: 35 minutes \ Servings: 4)

Ingredients:

1 cup black lentils, soaked

½ cup sour cream

2 tomatoes, chopped

¼ cup corn kernels

½ teaspoon chili powder

2-3 garlic cloves, minced

½ teaspoon salt

2 cups water

4 tablespoons cooking oil

¼ cup spinach, chopped

3 tablespoons lemon juice

3-4 corn tortillas

Directions:

Adjust the instant pot on pressure cook mode. Transfer the lentils with garlic, chili powder, oil, and water in instant pot. Cover and let it boil for 20 minutes. Place a tortilla and top with 1-2 tablespoons of cooked lentil, tomatoes, spinach and sour cream.

Repeat the steps for all tortillas. Drizzle lemon juice. Serve and enjoy.

59. Potato Curry with Peas

(Time: 40 minutes \ Servings: 5)

Ingredients:

1 cup peas

3 potatoes, peeled, cut into slices

¼ teaspoon turmeric powder

2-3 garlic cloves, minced

½ teaspoon salt

¼ teaspoon black pepper

2 cups water

Directions:

Set the instant pot on sauté mode. Heat oil and fry garlic for 30-40 seconds. Add peas and potatoes, fry until lightly golden with few splashes of water.

Add turmeric powder, salt, black pepper, water and cover the pot with a lid. Cook on pressure cook mode for 30 minutes. Serve and enjoy.

60. Stir Fried Garlic Zest Spinach

(Time: 25 minutes \ Servings: 3)

Ingredients:

2 cups baby spinach

3-4 garlic cloves, thinly sliced

¼ teaspoon salt

½ cup chicken stock

4 tablespoons butter

Directions:

Set the instant pot on sauté mode, melt butter and fry garlic for 20 seconds. Now add spinach and stir fry for 10 minutes. Add in chicken stock and mix thoroughly.

When water is dried out season the spinach with salt and pepper.

Serve and enjoy.

61. Spiced Stir fried Chickpeas

(Time: 15 minutes \ Servings: 3)

Ingredients:

2 cups chickpeas, boiled

4 tablespoons tamarind pulp

¼ teaspoon salt

¼ teaspoon black pepper

¼ teaspoon cumin powder

½ teaspoon cinnamon powder

1 teaspoon vinegar

1 tablespoons olive oil

Directions:

Heat oil in the instant pot on sauté mode. Add in chickpeas and stir fry for 2-3 minutes.

Add in tamarind pulp, salt, pepper, cumin powder, cinnamon powder, vinegar and fry for another 5-10 minutes. Serve and enjoy.

62. Chicken Stock

(Time: 45 minutes \ Servings: 5)

Ingredients:

½ lb. chicken

2 onions, halved

1 cup celery stems

4-5 garlic cloves

½ teaspoon black pepper

1 pinch turmeric powder

½ teaspoon salt

4 cups water

2 tablespoons cooking oil

Directions:

In the instant pot, add all ingredients and cook on stew mode for 50-60 minutes. Drain out stock and pour to serving bowls and serve hot. Serve and enjoy.

63. Sweet Potato Casserole

(Time: 45 minutes \ Servings: 4)

Ingredients:

4-5 sweet potatoes, boiled

½ teaspoon ginger powder

½ cup brown sugar

1 pinch salt

½ cup cream milk

3 eggs

4 tablespoons butter, melted

Directions:

Transfer the boiled sweet potatoes, salt, milk, brown sugar, ginger powder and blend until smooth.

Crack eggs in blender and blend for another 1 minute. Grease the instant pot with butter and transfer the sweet potatoes mixture, cover with a lid and cook for 40-45 minutes on slow cook mode.

Serve and enjoy.

64. Tuna Pasta Braise

(Time: 35 minutes \ Servings: 3)

Ingredients:

½ lb. tuna

1 package pasta, boiled

½ cup mayonnaise

½ cup sour cream

½ teaspoon salt

1 teaspoon black pepper

4-5 garlic cloves, minced

2 oz. cheddar cheese, shredded

2 tablespoons butter

Directions:

In the instant add butter and let it melt on sauté mode. Add in tuna and stir fry for 4-5 minutes. Add in garlic powder, salt, pepper, mozzarella cheese, sour cream, and mayonnaise, combine well.

Now add the pasta and cover the pot with a lid. Set the instant pot on slow stew mode and leave to cook for 20 minutes. Serve hot and enjoy.

65. Creamy Spinach Pulverize

(Time: 35 minutes \ Servings: 3)

Ingredients:

3 cups spinach, chopped

1 cup heavy cream

¼ teaspoon salt

1 teaspoon black pepper

1 onion, chopped

4-5 garlic cloves, minced

1 cup chicken stock

2 tablespoons butter

Directions:

In the instant add butter and let it melt on sauté mode. Sauté onion for 1 minute with garlic.

Now add spinach and simmer until lightly softened. Add in chicken stock, salt, pepper, creamy and mix well. Transfer this mixture to a blender and blend until puree. Pour the blended spinach back into the instant pot and cook for 15 minutes on slow cook mode. Serve hot and enjoy.

66. Hot Stir Fried Chili Pepper

(Time: 35 minutes \ Servings: 3)

Ingredients:

2 green bell peppers, sliced

2 red bell peppers, fried

1 onion, sliced

½ teaspoon salt

½ teaspoon chili powder

½ teaspoon garlic paste

2 tablespoons olive oil

Directions:

In the instant heat oil and on sauté mode. Add in onion with garlic, and fry until onion is transparent.

Add salt, chili powder, bell peppers and fry well. Stir fry for 10-15 minutes with few splashes of water.

Transfer to a serving dish and serve.

67. Creamy Sausage Pasta Casserole

(Time: 35 minutes \ Servings: 4)

Ingredients:

¼ lb. sausage, pieces

1 onion, chopped

¼ cup parmesan cheese, grated

¼ cup cheddar cheese

1 package pasta, boiled

½ teaspoon salt

1 teaspoon black pepper

1 teaspoon garlic paste

2 tablespoons olive oil

3 tablespoons tomato ketchup

1 cup cream milk

Directions:

Heat oil in instant pot on sauté mode, add onion and sauté for 1 minute. Add garlic with sausage and stir for 2 minutes. Season with salt and black pepper. Pour milk and let it simmer for 5 minutes.

Transfer the boiled pasta, ketchup, parmesan cheese, cheddar cheese, stir and cover with a lid. Let it cook for 20-25 minutes. Serve and enjoy.

68. Creamy Mashed Potatoes Simmer

(Time: 45 minutes \ Servings: 4)

Ingredients:

4 potatoes, boiled, peeled

1 cup cream milk

4 oz. mozzarella cheese

¼ teaspoon salt

1 teaspoon black pepper

½ cup parmesan cheese, shredded

2 garlic cloves, minced

2 tablespoons butter

Directions:

Set the instant pot on sauté mode. Add butter, onion, garlic and sauté for 1-2 minute.

In a bowl add potatoes, parmesan cheese, cream, mozzarella cheese, salt, black pepper, and mash with potato masher. Transfer this mixture to the instant pot and cover with a lid.

Cook on slow cook mode for 30-40 minutes. Serve and enjoy.

69. Instant Pot Fried Potatoes

(Time: 35 minutes \ Servings: 3)

Ingredients:

4 potatoes, peeled, thinly sliced

½ teaspoon chili flakes

¼ teaspoon salt

¼ teaspoon turmeric powder

2 tablespoons olive oil

Directions:

Adjust the instant pot on sauté mode. Add potatoes and fry for 5-10 minutes. Season with turmeric, salt and chili flakes. Cook on low heat for 10-15 minutes. Transfer to a serving dish and enjoy.

70. Mango Mash with Potatoes

(Time: 35 minutes \ Servings: 3)

Ingredients:

4 potatoes, boiled, peeled

1 cup mango, chunks

1 cup sour cream

1 avocado, pulp

½ cup mango juice

¼ teaspoon salt

1 teaspoon black pepper

2 garlic cloves, minced

2 tablespoons olive oil

Directions:

Set the instant pot on slow cook mode.

Transfer olive oil, mangos, avocado, cream, potatoes, salt, black pepper, mango juice, and garlic to the pot and cover with a lid.

Let it prepare for 35 minutes.

Serve and enjoy.

71. Chicken Potato Puffs

(Time: 35 minutes \ Servings: 4)

Ingredients:

2 potatoes, boiled, peeled

1 cup chicken cubes, boiled

¼ teaspoon garlic paste

¼ teaspoon salt

¼ teaspoon cumin powder

½ teaspoon chili flakes

1 onion, chopped

2 puff pastry sheets, cut into 3-4 small squares

¼ cup water

2 tablespoons cooking oil

Directions:

Set the instant pot on sauté mode. Heat oil and fry garlic with chicken and potatoes until lightly golden. Season with cumin powder, salt and chili flakes. Now transfer this mixture to a bowl.

Spread puff pastry square and top with 3-4 tablespoons of chicken mixture, lift the sides of square and place over the stuffing. Place to a greased instant pot and cook for 25 minutes on pressure cook mode. Serve with chili garlic sauce and enjoy.

72. Chicken Spinach Beef Stew

(Time: 55 minutes \ Servings: 6)

Ingredients:

½ lb. beef, pieces

1 chicken breast, cut into pieces

1 cup spinach, sliced

2 green chilies

1 cup tomato puree

¼ teaspoon garlic paste

1 onion, chopped

¼ teaspoon cumin powder

½ teaspoon black pepper

4 cups water

2 tablespoons cooking oil

Directions:

Set the instant pot on pressure cook mode. Add all ingredients and cook for 55 minutes. Serve with chili garlic sauce and enjoy.

73. Stir Fried Garlic Mushroom

(Time: 35 minutes \ Servings: 4)

Ingredients:

2 cups mushrooms, sliced

2 tablespoons soya sauce

2 tablespoons oyster sauce

¼ teaspoon garlic paste

¼ teaspoon salt

1 cup baby corns

½ teaspoons black pepper

2 tablespoons coconut oil

2 tablespoons cilantro, chopped

¼ cup chicken broth

Directions:

Set the instant pot on sauté mode. Heat oil and fry garlic with mushrooms for 10 minutes. Season with, broth, corns, oyster sauce, soya sauce, salt and pepper. Let it cook for 20 minutes. Sprinkle cilantro on top. Fry for 10-15 minutes. Transfer to a serving dish and enjoy.

74. Pineapple Lemonade Pilaf

(Time: 25 minutes \ Servings: 4)

Ingredients:

1 cup rice, soaked

1 cup pineapple juice

1 cup water

1 teaspoon salt

1 cup pineapple chunks

3 tablespoons lemon juice

½ teaspoon black pepper

1 onion, chopped

2 tablespoons cooking oil

Few pineapple slice

1 lime slice

Directions:

Set the instant pot on sauté mode. Heat oil and fry onion until softened. Add pineapple juice, water, lemon juice, salt and pepper; let it boil. Now add in rice, pineapple chunks and let it boil well.

Cover with a lid and prepare on rice mode for 20 minutes. Transfer to a serving dish and garnish with pineapple and lime slices. Enjoy.

75. Spiced Zucchini Fingers

(Time: 15 minutes \ Servings: 5)

Ingredients:

2 large zucchinis, sliced

1 teaspoon cumin powder

1 teaspoon cinnamon power

¼ teaspoon garlic powder

¼ teaspoon salt

2 tablespoons all-purpose flour

½ teaspoon chili powder

½ cup cooking oil, for frying.

Directions:

Roll out zucchini slices into flour, place aside.

Set the instant pot on sauté mode.

Heat oil and deep fry zucchini until lightly golden.

Spread to a paper towel and drain out excess oil.

Combine salt, chili powder, cinnamon powder, cumin powder, and sprinkle over zucchini.

Serve and enjoy.

76. Instant Pot Zucchini Chips

(Time: 15 minutes \ Servings: 4)

Ingredients:

3 large zucchinis, thinly sliced

¼ teaspoon salt

¼ teaspoon black pepper

½ tablespoons cooking oil, for frying

Directions:

Heat oil in the instant pot on sauté mode. Transfer a few slices of zucchini in the instant pot and fry until nicely golden and crispy. Repeat the same steps for all zucchini chips.

Then place onto a paper towel and drain out the excessive oil. Season with salt and pepper. Serve and enjoy.

77. Roasted Fennel with Tomatoes

(Time: 35 minutes \ Servings: 3)

Ingredients:

4-5 fennel bulbs, timed and quartered

3 Cherry tomatoes

1 pinch of caraway seed

1 tablespoon olive oil

¼ teaspoon salt

¼ teaspoon red chili flakes

2 cups vegetable broth

Directions:

Place the funnel bulbs inside the instant pot with tomatoes and olive oil. Add all remaining ingredients. Cook on slow cook mode until funnels become tender. Serve and enjoy.

78. Thyme Zest Potato Mash

(Time: 35 minutes \ Servings: 5)

Ingredients:

4 baking potatoes

1 teaspoon salt

1 teaspoon black pepper

1 teaspoon garlic paste/powder

4 tablespoons olive oil

3 sprigs of fresh thyme

Directions:

Peel and wash potatoes. Prick potatoes a bit with fork. Drizzle a few drops of oil on the potatoes and place in the instant pot, let it cook for 20-25 minutes on pressure cook mode. Then, put them in a large bowl and add all remaining ingredients, mash with a fork. Sprinkle black paper on top and serve.

79. Instant Pot Spinach and Potato Risotto

(Time: 45 minutes \ Servings: 5)

Ingredients:

2 cups spinach, chopped

¼ cup mushrooms, sliced

2 large potatoes, peeled, diced

1 onion, chopped

2-3 cherry tomatoes, halved

½ teaspoon salt

¼ teaspoons turmeric powder

1 teaspoon chili flakes

½ teaspoon cumin powder

½ teaspoon garlic paste

3 tablespoons cooking oil

2 cups water

Directions:

Heat oil in the instant pot on sauté mode. Fry onion until transparent. Add mushrooms, garlic, salt, chili flakes, turmeric powder, and fry. Now add spinach and stir with some splashes of water.

Add water, the potatoes and cover with a lid. Cook on manual mode for 35 minutes. Stir in cherry tomatoes and cook for 1-2 minutes. Turn off flame when potatoes are tendered and water is dried out. Sprinkle cumin powder and mix well. Serve and enjoy.

80. Asparagus Chowder

(Time: 45 minutes \ Servings: 5)

Ingredients:

1 tablespoon olive oil

2 cups chopped onion

2 teaspoons grated lemon rind

1 cup boiled rice

3 cans fat-free, less-sodium chicken broth

2 cups sliced asparagus

2 cups chopped spinach

¼ teaspoon ground nutmeg

½ cup grated fresh Parmesan cheese

½ teaspoon salt

Directions:

Heat oil in the instant pot, add onion, stir for 5 minutes until transparent.

Now add rice, lemon rind, asparagus, spinach, chicken broth, salt and cook for 10 minutes with covered lid on slow flame.

Turn off heat. Add Parmesan cheese and sprinkle ground nutmeg. Serve and enjoy.

81. Slow Cooked Cabbage

(Time: 45 minutes \ Servings: 5)

Ingredients:

4-5 baby cabbages, halved

1 teaspoon salt

1 cup tomato sauce

2 tablespoon olive oil

¼ teaspoon white pepper

½ teaspoon slat

Directions:

In the instant pot add all and toss well. Add tomato sauce. Let it cook on slow cook mode for 60 minutes.

Transfer the cabbages to a serving platter and enjoy.

82. Roasted Fennel with Carrots

(Time: 35 minutes \ Servings: 3)

Ingredients:

4-5 fennel bulbs, timed and quartered

3 carrots, shredded

1 pinch of caraway seed

1 tablespoon olive oil

¼ teaspoon salt

¼ teaspoon red chili flakes

Directions:

In the instant pot add all and toss well. Add tomato sauce. Let it cook on slow cook mode for 60 minutes.

Transfer the cabbages to a serving platter and enjoy.

83. Eggplant and Tomato Instant Pot Curry

(Time: 25 minutes \ Servings: 4)

Ingredients:

3 eggplant, cut into small pieces

1 onion, chopped

3 large tomatoes, chopped

½ teaspoon salt

1 teaspoon chili powder

¼ teaspoon turmeric powder

½ teaspoon garlic paste

½ teaspoon ginger paste

¼ cup cooking oil

Directions:

Heat oil in the instant pot on sauté mode. Add eggplant and fry until nicely golden, transfer to a platter and place aside. Now in the same oil sauté onion until transparent.

Add in tomatoes, salt, chili powder, turmeric powder, ginger garlic paste and fry well. Add the fried eggplants and cook for 10-14 minutes on high heat. Serve and enjoy.

84. Chili and Garlic Zest Pumpkin

(Time: 35 minutes \ Servings: 3)

Ingredients:

2 cups pumpkin, cut into small slices

3 green chilies, chopped

¼ teaspoon salt

1 teaspoon chili powder

¼ teaspoon turmeric powder

½ teaspoon garlic paste

2 tablespoons cooking oil

Directions:

Heat oil in the instant pot on sauté mode. Fry garlic with green chilies for a minute.

Add in salt, chili powder, turmeric powder and stir. Now add in pumpkin slices and fry on high heat for 10-15 minutes. Cover with a lid and let it cook on low heat for another 10-15 minutes on slow cook mode.Transfer to a serving dish. Serve and enjoy.

85. Carrot and Pumpkin Stew

(Time: 60 minutes \ Servings: 4)

Ingredients:

1 cup pumpkin, chopped

1 onion, chopped

4 carrot, peeled, chopped

1 teaspoon salt

1 teaspoon black pepper

½ teaspoon cumin powder

3-4 garlic cloves, minced

2 tablespoons olive oil

2 cups chicken broth

1 cup vegetable broth

Directions:

In the instant pot add pumpkin, carrots, chicken broth, onion, oil, salt, garlic, cumin powder, vegetable broth, black pepper and mix well. Cover the pot with a lid and let it prepare the food on slow cook mode for 60 minutes. Transfer to a blender and blend until puree.

Pour the stew into serving bowls and serve hot. Enjoy.

86. Peas and Carrots with Potatoes

(Time: 40 minutes \ Servings: 5)

Ingredients:

1 cup peas

1 cup cauliflower florets

3 potatoes, small cubes

2 carrots, peeled, cut into small cubes

1 onion, chopped

1 teaspoon salt

1 teaspoon chili powder

1.4 teaspoon turmeric powder

½ teaspoon cumin powder

2 tomatoes chopped

½ teaspoon cinnamon powder

½ teaspoon garlic paste

2 tablespoons cooking oil

1 cup water

Directions:

Heat oil in the instant pot on sauté mode, sauté onion until transparent. Add in tomatoes, salt, chili powder, turmeric powder, ginger garlic paste and fry well. Add all vegetables and fry for 10-15 minutes on high heat.

Now add the water and cover with a lid. Let it simmer for 15 minutes. Serve with boiled rice.

87. Slow Cooked Honey Glazed Carrots

(Time: 45 minutes \ Servings: 5)

Ingredients:

1 oz. carrots, peeled

1 tablespoon red wine vinegar

2 tablespoons of unsalted butte

1 teaspoon black pepper

1 pinch salt

1 cup water

½ cup brown sugar

2 tablespoon honey

Directions:

In the instant pot add all ingredients except the honey and let it cook on slow cook mode for 60 minutes. Transfer to a serving platter and drizzle honey on top. Serve and enjoy.

88. Tropic Cauliflower Manchurian

(Time: 35 minutes \ Servings: 4)

Ingredients:

2 cups cauliflower florets

1 onion, chopped

1 teaspoon salt

1 teaspoon chili flakes

½ teaspoon cumin powder

3 green chilies, sliced

1 cup tomato puree

3 tablespoons tomato ketchup

½ teaspoon cinnamon powder

½ teaspoon garlic paste

¼ teaspoon turmeric powder

¼ cup cooking oil

Directions:

Heat oil in the instant pot on sauté mode. Add cauliflower florets and fry until lightly golden, put to a platter and set aside. Now in the same pot sauté onion until transparent.

Add in tomato puree, tomato ketchup, salt, chili flakes, turmeric powder, garlic paste and fry for 5-6 minutes. Add cauliflower and fry again for 4-5 minutes on high heat. Sprinkle cinnamon powder, cumin powder and green chilies on top. Serve and enjoy.

89. Garlic Fried Mushrooms

(Time: 15 minutes \ Servings: 3)

Ingredients:

2 cups mushrooms, sliced

¼ teaspoon salt

1 teaspoon black pepper

½ teaspoon garlic paste

2 tablespoons soya sauce

1 teaspoon basil, chopped

2 tablespoons cooking oil

Directions:

Heat oil on sauté mode. Fry garlic for 30 seconds. Stir in mushrooms and fry for 5-10 minutes on medium flame. Now add in soya sauce and combine well.

Season with salt and pepper. Let it cook for 5 minutes, stir occasionally. Sprinkle basil on top. Serve and enjoy.

90. Instant Pot Rice with Carrot

(Time: 35 minutes \ Servings: 4)

Ingredients:

2 cups rice, soaked

2 carrots, peeled, chopped

1 potatoes, peeled, chopped

1 teaspoon cumin seeds

1 black cardamom

2-3 cinnamon sticks

1 tomato, sliced

2 large onions, sliced

1 teaspoon salt

4 tablespoons olive oil

4 cups vegetables broth

Directions:

Heat oil on sauté mode. Fry onion with cumin seeds, cinnamon sticks, and cardamom, until nicely golden. Add carrots, potatoes, salt, chili powder, and fry.

Then add the tomato slices and pour in vegetable broth, let it boil. Add rice and when bubbles appear on top cover the pot with a lid. Let it cook on medium heat for 20-25 minutes. Transfer to a serving dish and enjoy.

91. Tropic Potato Gravy

(Time: 25 minutes \ Servings: 4)

Ingredients:

4 potatoes, boiled, peeled, cut into cubes

1 onion, chopped

1 teaspoon cumin seeds

1 teaspoon chili powder

½ teaspoon cumin powder

1 cup tomato puree

½ teaspoon cinnamon powder

½ teaspoon garlic paste

½ teaspoon thyme

¼ teaspoon turmeric powder

2 tablespoons cooking oil

½ cup chicken broth

Directions:

Heat oil in the instant pot on sauté mode sauté onion with cumin seeds, and garlic for 1 minute. Add in tomato puree, salt, chili powder, turmeric powder, garlic paste and fry for 5-6 minutes. Add potatoes and mix thoroughly. Stir in chicken broth and cook for 10 minutes on medium flame.

Sprinkle cinnamon powder, thyme and cumin powder on top. Serve and enjoy.

92. Crispy Kale Chips
(Time: 10 minutes \ Servings: 4)

Ingredients:

2 cups kale leaves, halved

¼ teaspoon salt

¼ teaspoon black pepper

½ teaspoon garlic powder

½ tablespoons cooking oil, for frying

Directions:

Heat oil in the instant pot on sauté mode. Deep fry some kale leave until nicely golden and crispy.

Repeat the steps for all kale leaves.Place to a paper towel and let the excessive oil drain out. Season with garlic powder, salt and pepper. Serve and enjoy.

93. Ground Beef Zucchini Zoodles
(Time: 35 minutes \ Servings: 4)

Ingredients:

¼ lb. beef mince

1 large zucchinis, spiraled

1 onion, chopped

2 tablespoons olive oil

2 tomatoes, chopped

2-3 garlic cloves, minced

½ teaspoon black pepper

¼ teaspoon chili powder

2 tablespoons soya sauce

1 oz. parmesan cheese, gated

¼ teaspoon salt

Directions:

Heat oil on sauté mode. Fry onion for a minute with garlic. Now add the beef and fry util nicely brown. Add in the tomatoes, salt, chili powder, soya sauce, and pepper.

Transfer the fried ground beef to a bowl and place aside. Now in the same pot add zucchini zoodles and fry for 5-10 minutes. Now transfer the fried ground beef and combine. Sprinkle cheese on top. Serve and enjoy.

94. Spinach Black Bean Chili

(Time: 45 minutes \ Servings: 4)

Ingredients:

2 cans of black beans

2 tomatoes, chopped

1 cup spinach, chopped

1 cup red bell pepper, chopped

2 large onions, chopped

1 teaspoon salt

3 garlic cloves, minced

2 tablespoons olive oil

4 cups vegetables broth

½ teaspoon black pepper

1 teaspoon red chili powder

1 bunch coriander, chopped

2 tablespoons sour cream

2 green chilies, chopped

Directions:

In the instant pot, add all ingredients, stir and cover with a lid. Cook on slow cook mode for 2-3 hours. Transfer to a serving dish and sprinkle coriander. Top with sour cream. Serve and enjoy.

95. Instant Pot Mashed Potato Pilaf

(Time: 45 minutes \ Servings: 5)

Ingredients:

2 cups rice, soaked

3 potatoes, boiled, mashed

1 teaspoon cumin seeds

1 carrot, peeled, chopped

1 bay leaf

2 garlic cloves, minced

2 cloves

1 tomato, chopped

2 large onions, sliced

1 teaspoon salt

4 tablespoons olive oil

4 cups vegetables broth

Directions:

Heat oil in the instant pot on sauté mode. Fry onion with cumin seeds, bay leaf and cloves until nicely brown. Now add in the potatoes, carrots, salt, chili powder, garlic and fry.

Add in tomatoes, and stir fry until potatoes are softened. Pour in vegetable broth and let it boil. Add rice and when bubbles appear on top cover the pot. Cook on medium heat for 20 minutes on rice mode. Transfer to a serving dish and enjoy.

96. Stir Fried Vegetables

(Time: 15 minutes \ Servings: 4)

Ingredients:

2 green bell peppers
1 yellow bell pepper
1 zucchini, sliced
1 onion, sliced
½ cup mushrooms, sliced
¼ teaspoon salt

¼ teaspoon chili powder
½ teaspoon garlic paste
2 tablespoons soya sauce
2 tablespoons vinegar
2 tablespoons oil

Directions:

Heat oil in the instant pot on sauté mode and stir fry all vegetables with garlic. Season with salt, pepper, and soya sauce. Cover with a lid and cook for 5-10 minutes or until vegetables are softened.

97. Instant Pot Pees Pilaf

(Time: 45 minutes \ Servings: 5)

Ingredients:

2 cups rice, soaked
1 cup peas
1 teaspoon cumin seeds
1 bay leaf
2 garlic cloves, minced
1 pinch turmeric powder
1 teaspoon cumin powder

1 teaspoon cinnamon powder
2 tomatoes, chopped
2 medium onions, sliced
1 teaspoon salt
3 tablespoons olive oil
4 cups chicken broth

Directions:

Heat oil in the instant pot on sauté mode, fry onion with cumin seeds, and bay leaf until nicely brown. Now add peas, salt, turmeric powder, chili powder, garlic and fry.

Add in tomatoes, and stir fry.

Pour in vegetable broth and add cumin powder, cinnamon powder, let it boil. Add rice, let it simmer until you see bubbles, then cover up the pot with a lid.

Let it cook on medium heat for 20 minutes on rice mode. Transfer to a serving dish and enjoy

98. Eggplant and Potato Gravy

(Time: 55 minutes \ Servings: 5)

Ingredients:

2 eggplant, sliced

2 potatoes, peeled, diced

1 onion, chopped

3 large tomatoes, chopped

½ teaspoon salt

1 teaspoon chili powder

¼ teaspoon dry coriander powder

¼ teaspoon turmeric powder

½ teaspoon garlic paste

2 tablespoons cooking oil

Directions:

Heat oil in the instant pot on sauté mode and sauté onion until transparent.

Add in tomatoes, salt, chili powder, turmeric powder, garlic paste and fry well.

Add eggplants and fry for 15 minutes on high heat. Now add potatoes and fry continuously, add few splashes of water while frying. Cover with a lid and cook on low heat for 10-15 minutes.

Sprinkle cumin powder and mix thoroughly.

Serve and enjoy.

99. Instant Pot Cabbage with Potatoes

(Time: 35 minutes \ Servings: 5)

Ingredients:

1 cup cabbage, chopped

2 potatoes, sliced

1 onion, chopped

2 tomatoes, chopped

½ teaspoon salt

1 teaspoon chili powder

¼ teaspoon turmeric powder

½ teaspoon garlic paste

2-3 green chilies, chopped

2 tablespoons cooking oil

Directions:

Heat oil in the instant pot on sauté mode, sauté onion until transparent. Add in tomatoes, salt, chili powder, turmeric powder, garlic paste and fry for 5-10 minutes. Transfer cabbage and fry well.

Add potatoes, and stir well until the potatoes are softened. Let it cook on low heat for 10-15 minutes. Serve and enjoy.

100. Cauliflower with Carrot Stew

(Time: 35 minutes \ Servings: 4)

Ingredients:

2 cups cauliflower florets

1 cup green beans

2 carrots, sliced

1 onion, chopped

1 cup spinach

1 teaspoon salt

1 teaspoon black pepper

1 bay leaf

½ teaspoon cumin powder

½ teaspoon garlic paste

1 ginger slice

2 tablespoons cooking oil

Directions:

In the instant pot add all ingredients and stir, cover with a lid. Set the instant pot on stew mode and let it prepare. Put to a serving dish and serve hot. Enjoy it.

Instant Pot Soup Recipes

101. Instant Pot Tomato Gravy Soup

(Time: 55 minutes \ Servings: 4)

Ingredients:

1 cup tomato puree

2 tablespoons chili garlic sauce

2 cups chicken broth

1 garlic clove minced

1 red chili

¼ teaspoon salt

¼ teaspoon black pepper

2 tablespoons cooking oil

Directions:

In the instant pot, add the tomato puree, chicken broth, salt, pepper, garlic, chili, chili garlic sauce, oil, and stir well. Cover with a lid and cook on stew mode for 40 minutes. Transfer the soup to a blender and blend it.

Transfer to the pot again and let it simmer for 5 minutes. Pour to a serving dish and serve.

102. Pumpkin and Potato Soup

(Time: 55 minutes \ Servings: 4)

Ingredients:

1 cup pumpkin chunks, peeled

2 potatoes, cut into small cubes

2 cups vegetable broth

1 cup milk

2 tablespoons fish sauce

¼ teaspoon turmeric powder

½ teaspoon chili powder

4-5 garlic cloves, minced

¼ teaspoon salt

1 tablespoon oil

Directions:

Heat oil in the instant pot and add garlic cloves, cook for 1 minute.

Add the pumpkin with potatoes and cook for 5 minutes. Stir in vegetable broth, salt, chili powder, turmeric powder, fish sauce and mix; cook on low heat for 20 minutes on stew mode.

Now add milk and cook for another 5 minutes. Turn off the heat and ladle the soup into serving bowls.Enjoy.

103. Cauliflower Soup

(Time: 55 minutes \ Servings: 4)

Ingredients:

1 cup cauliflower florets

1 teaspoon ginger paster

1 red bell pepper chopped

2 cups vegetable broth

2 tablespoons vinegar

1 lemon, sliced

1 green chili, chopped

4-5 garlic cloves, minced

½ teaspoon black pepper

¼ teaspoon salt

1 tablespoon oil

Directions:

Heat oil in the instant pot, add the ginger paste and cook for 1 minute on sauté mode. Add cauliflower and fry well for 5-10 minutes. Now add bell pepper, salt, pepper, vinegar, green chilies, lemon slices and mix well.

Add vegetable broth and cook on medium heat for 15 minutes on stew mode. Pour into serving bowls. Enjoy.

104. Peas and Spinach Soup

(Time: 45 minutes \ Servings: 4)

Ingredients:

1 cup baby spinach

1 cup peas

2 cups vegetable broth

½ cup milk

4-5 garlic cloves, minced

1 cup cream

½ cup tofu

½ teaspoon chili flakes

¼ teaspoon salt

2 tablespoons oil

Directions:

Heat oil in the saucepan and add garlic cloves, cook for 1 minute on sauté mode. Add vegetable broth, spinach, peas, tofu, cream, chili flake, and salt, mix well. Let it cook on medium heat for 10 minutes on stew mode.

Pour in milk and cook for 5 minutes on low heat. Pour into serving bowls. Enjoy.

105. Coriander and Spinach Soup

(Time: 45 minutes \ Servings: 4)

Ingredients:

1 cup baby spinach

1 bunch coriander, puree

2 cups vegetable broth

1 cup heavy cream

½ cup milk

4-5 garlic cloves, minced

½ teaspoon chili flakes

¼ teaspoon salt

2 tablespoons oil

Directions:

Heat oil in the saucepan and add garlic cloves, cook for 1 minute on sauté mode. Add vegetable broth, spinach, coriander puree, cream, chili flake, and salt, mix well.

Let it cook on medium heat for 10 minutes on stew mode. Pour in milk and cook for 5 minutes on low heat. Spoon into serving bowls. Serve and enjoy.

106. Shrimps Soup

(Time: 35 minutes \ Servings: 4)

Ingredients:

1 oz. shrimps

2 cups chicken broth

¼ cup apple cider vinegar

4-5 garlic cloves, minced

½ teaspoon black pepper

¼ teaspoon salt

1 tablespoon oil

2 tomatoes, sliced

Directions:

Heat oil and add garlic cloves, fry for 1 minute. Add shrimps and fry for 10 minutes. Season with salt and pepper. Add chicken broth, tomatoes, vinegar and stir well. Let it cook on medium heat for 10 minutes on stew mode. Pour into serving bowls. Serve and enjoy.

107. Instant Pot Chicken Corn Soup

(Time: 45 minutes \ Servings: 3)

Ingredients:

1 cup chicken, boiled, shredded
¼ cup water
2 tablespoons corn flour
3 cups chicken broth

1 garlic clove minced
¼ teaspoon salt
¼ teaspoon black pepper
2 tablespoons cooking oil

Directions:

Heat oil in the instant pot and fry garlic for 30 seconds. Add shredded chicken and stir fry. Add chicken broth and cook on low heat for 20 minutes on stew mode. Combine corn flour with water and pour gradually into the soup until thickened.

Season the soup with salt and pepper. Ladle to a serving dish and serve.

108. Chickpea and Basil Soup

(Time: 35 minutes \ Servings: 3)

Ingredients:

1 cup chickpeas, boiled
2-3 basil leaves
3 cups vegetable broth
1 garlic clove minced

¼ teaspoon salt
¼ teaspoon chili powder
¼ teaspoon black pepper
2 tablespoons cooking oil

Directions:

In the instant pot, add all ingredients and cook on stew mode. Transfer to serving bowls and serve hot. Enjoy.

109. Sweet and Sour Tomato Soup

(Time: 35 minutes \ Servings: 3)

Ingredients:

1 cup tomato sauce

½ cup tomato ketchup

2 cups vegetable broth

¼ cup water

3 tablespoons of corn flour

2 tablespoons vinegar

2 garlic cloves, minced

4 tablespoons brown sugar

½ teaspoon black pepper

¼ teaspoon salt

1 tablespoon oil

Directions:

Set the instant pot on sauté mode. Heat oil inside it and add garlic cloves, sauté for 1 minute. Add tomato puree, tomato ketchup, vinegar and fry for 1-2 minutes. Add in vegetable broth, and season with salt, sugar and pepper. Let it simmer for 20-25 minutes on stew mode.

Combine water with corn flour and mix well. Gradually add this mixture into soup and stir continuously for 1-2 minutes. Pour into serving bowls and enjoy.

110. Vegetable Soup

(Time: 30 minutes \ Servings: 3)

Ingredients:

1 cup broccoli florets

1 green bell pepper, sliced

1 red bell pepper, sliced

1 carrot, sliced

1 onion, sliced

2 cups vegetable broth

1 tablespoons lemon juice

4-5 garlic cloves, minced

½ teaspoon black pepper

¼ teaspoon salt

1 tablespoons cooking oil

Directions:

Set the instant pot on sauté mode. Heat oil in the instant, add onion and garlic cloves, sauté for 1 minute. Add all vegetables, stir fry and let it cook on low heat for 5-10 minutes. Add vegetable broth, salt, pepper and mix well.

Let it cook on stew mode for 15 minutes. Drizzle lemon juice. Ladle into serving bowls and enjoy.

111. Spicy Noodle Chicken Soup

(Time: 25 minutes \ Servings: 4)

Ingredients:

1 oz. chicken, boiled, cubes

1 onion, sliced

1 package noodles, cooked

3 cups chicken broth

2 tablespoons vinegar

4-5 garlic cloves, minced

½ teaspoon black pepper

¼ teaspoon salt

1 tablespoon oil

Directions:

Heat oil in the instant pot and add garlic cloves with onion, cook for 1 minute on sauté mode. Add the chicken with carrots and fry for 5 minutes. Stir in the chicken broth, vinegar, salt and pepper.

Add the noodles and cook on 15 minutes on stew mode. Ladle to serving bowls. Serve and enjoy.

112. Garlic Chicken and Egg Soup

(Time: 35 minutes \ Servings: 3)

Ingredients:

2 oz. chicken, cut into small pieces

1 onion, chopped

2 eggs, whisked

2 cups chicken broth

¼ cup water

3 tablespoons of flour

4-5 garlic cloves, minced

½ teaspoon black pepper

¼ teaspoon salt

1 tablespoon oil

Directions:

Heat oil in the instant pot on sauté mode, sauté garlic with onion for 1 minute. Now add the chicken and fry for 10 minutes. Shred it and transfer it to the instant pot again.

Season with black pepper, salt and mix well. Add the chicken broth, simmer for 15 minutes on stew mode. In a bowl add water with corn flour and mix well.

Gradually pour this mixture into soup and stir continuously for 2 minutes. Add the eggs by gradually sting soup. Cook for another 2 minutes. Ladle into bowls and enjoy.

113. Pumpkin Purée Soup

(Time: 35 minutes \ Servings: 3)

Ingredients:

2 cups pumpkin puree

2 cups vegetable broth

1 cup cream milk

2 tablespoons soya sauce

¼ teaspoon turmeric powder

½ teaspoon black pepper

4-5 garlic cloves, minced

¼ teaspoon salt

1 tablespoon oil

Directions:

Heat oil in the instant pot and add garlic cloves, cook for 1 minute on sauté mode.

Add pumpkin and fry for 5 minutes.

Stir in vegetable broth, salt, pepper, turmeric powder, soya sauce and mix, let it cook on low heat for 20 minutes on stew mode.

Now add milk and cook for another 5 minutes.

Ladle the soup into serving bowls.

Serve and enjoy.

114. Bell Pepper and Cabbage Soup

(Time: 55 minutes \ Servings: 4)

Ingredients:

1 cup cabbages, shredded

1 red bell pepper, sliced

1 onion, sliced

2 cups chicken broth

1 tablespoon fish sauce

1 tablespoons lemon juice

4-5 garlic cloves, minced

½ teaspoon black pepper

¼ teaspoon salt

1 tablespoon oil

Directions:

Heat oil in the pot, add onion and cook for 1 minute on sauté mode. Add all garlic, bell pepper, cabbage and cook for 5 minutes. Add chicken broth, fish sauce, salt, pepper and mix well.

Let it cook on low heat for 15 minutes on stew mode. Add cream and cook for 5 minutes. Ladle into serving bowls. Drizzle lemon juice. Serve and enjoy.

115. Spinach Soup

(Time: 35 minutes \ Servings: 3)

Ingredients:

1 cup baby spinach

2 cups vegetable broth

½ cup milk

2 garlic cloves, minced

½ teaspoon chili flakes

¼ teaspoon salt

¼ cup sour cream

2 tablespoons oil

Directions:

In the instant pot, add all ingredients and cover with a lid. Set the pot on stew mode, let it cook for 25 minutes. Transfer to a blender and blend until creamy.

Pour spinach soup again into the pot and let it cook for another 6 minutes. Top with sour cream.

116. Cabbage Soup

(Time: 35 minutes \ Servings: 3)

Ingredients:

1 cup cabbage, chopped

2 cups chicken broth

2 garlic cloves, minced

½ teaspoon black pepper

2 tablespoons soya sauce

1 tablespoons vinegar

¼ teaspoon salt

2 tablespoons oil

Directions:

In the instant pot, add all ingredients and cover with a lid. Set the pot on stew mode, let it cook for 35 minutes. Serve and enjoy.

117. Onion and Carrot Soup

(Time: 35 minutes \ Servings: 3)

Ingredients:

1 onion, sliced

2 carrots, chopped

1 tablespoon fish sauce

2 cups chicken broth

1 egg, whisked

2 tablespoons vinegar

1 cup tomato puree

4-5 garlic cloves, minced

½ teaspoon black pepper

¼ teaspoon salt

1 tablespoon oil

Directions:

Heat oil in the instant pot and add garlic cloves with onion, cook for 1 minute on sauté mode. Stir in the carrots and cook for 2 minutes. Add soya sauce, salt, pepper, fish sauce and stir.

Add chicken broth, tomato puree, and leave to cook on low heat for 15 minutes on stew mode. Now add the egg and stir continuously. Ladle into serving bowls. Serve and enjoy..

118. Chickpea Broccoli Soup

(Time: 35 minutes \ Servings: 3)

Ingredients:

1 cup broccoli florets

1 cup chickpea, boiled

1medium onion, chopped

2 cups chicken broth

3 garlic cloves, minced

½ teaspoon black pepper

¼ teaspoon salt

2 tablespoons white rice vinegar

1 tablespoon oil

Directions:

Heat oil in the instant pot sauté garlic cloves for 1 minute on sauté mode. Stir in chickpeas, broccoli, onion, salt, pepper and sauté well. Pour in chicken broth, and vinegar, cook on low heat for 25 minutes on stew mode.

Transfer to a blender and blend till puree. Ladle into serving bowls. Serve and enjoy.

119. Rice Soup with Broccoli

(Time: 35 minutes \ Servings: 3)

Ingredients:

1 cup broccoli florets

1 cup rice, boiled

1 onion, sliced

2 cups vegetable broth

1 cup chicken broth

1 tablespoon lemon juice

2 garlic cloves, minced

½ teaspoon black pepper

¼ teaspoon salt

1 tablespoon oil

Directions:

In the instant pot, add all ingredients and stir. Adjust the pot on stew mode and cover up with a lid. Cook for 30-35 minutes on low flame. Bland soup well. Ladle the soup to bowls and serve hot.

Enjoy.

120. Yellow Lentils Hot Soup

(Time: 60 minutes \ Servings: 3)

Ingredients:

1 cup yellow lentils, soaked

1 cup water

¼ teaspoon turmeric powder

½ teaspoon ginger paste

1 onion, chopped

3 cups chicken broth

4-5 garlic cloves, minced

½ teaspoon chili powder

¼ teaspoon salt

2 tablespoon butter

Directions:

In the instant pot, add all ingredients and stir. Set the pot on slow cook mode and cover up with a lid. Cook for 60 minutes on low flame. Pour the soup into bowls and serve. Enjoy.

121. Red Beans Soup

(Time: 35 minutes \ Servings: 3)

Ingredients:

2 cup red beans, boiled

1 onion, sliced

1 tomato chopped

2 cups chicken broth

1 tablespoons lemon juice

4-5 garlic cloves, minced

½ teaspoon black pepper

¼ teaspoon salt

1 green chili, chopped

1 tablespoon oil

Directions:

Heat oil in the instant pot sauté garlic with onion for 1 minute on sauté mode. Stir in beans, chicken broth, salt, pepper, and green chili. Let it cook on manual mode for 30 minutes.

Ladle into serving bowls and drizzle lemon juice.

Serve and enjoy.

122. Potato Cream Soup

(Time: 35 minutes \ Servings: 3)

Ingredients:

4 large potatoes, boiled, mashed

1 onion, sliced

2 cups chicken broth

1 cup heavy cream

3 garlic cloves, minced

½ teaspoon black pepper

¼ teaspoon salt

1 tablespoon oil

Directions:

Heat oil in the instant pot, add onion and garlic cloves, cook for 1 minute on sauté mode. Add boiled potatoes and stir well. Stir in cream, chicken broth, salt, and pepper. Cook on low heat for 20 minutes on stew mode. Now remove from heat and let it cool a little bit.

Transfer into the food processor and blend until puree. Pour into the instant pot and cook for 5 minutes. Ladle into serving bowls and drizzle lemon juice. Serve and enjoy.

123. Spinach and Chickpea Soup

(Time: 65 minutes \ Servings: 4)

Ingredients:

1 cup chickpea

1 cup spinach, chopped

2 cups chicken broth

4-5 garlic cloves, minced

½ teaspoon black pepper

¼ teaspoon chili powder

¼ teaspoon salt

1 tablespoon oil

Directions:

Transfer all add all ingredients into the instant pot and stir. Set on slow cook mode and cover with a lid. Cook for 60-65 minutes on low flame. Ladle the soup to bowls and serve.

Enjoy.

124. Chicken Spaghetti Soup Curry

(Time: 35 minutes \ Servings: 3)

Ingredients:

1 onion, sliced

4 tablespoons tomato puree

1 cup chicken, boneless, cubes, boiled

1 package spaghetti, boiled

2 cups chicken broth

3 garlic cloves, minced

½ teaspoon chili powder

1 carrot, sliced

¼ teaspoon salt

1 tablespoon oil

Directions:

Heat oil in the instant pot, sauté onion and garlic for 1 minute on sauté mode. Stir in tomato puree for 1 minute.

Now add chicken pieces, carrot, spaghetti, chicken broth and cook on low heat for 20 minutes on stew mode. Season with salt and chili powder. Ladle into serving bowls. Serve and enjoy.

125. Mushroom Soup

(Time: 35 minutes \ Servings: 3)

Ingredients:

1 cup mushrooms, sliced

1 onion, sliced

1 cup chicken broth

3 garlic cloves, minced

¼ teaspoon ginger paste

½ teaspoon black pepper

¼ teaspoon salt

1 tablespoon oil

Directions:

Heat oil in the instant pot, add onion and garlic cloves, sauté for 1 minute on sauté mode. Add mushrooms with ginger paste and stir fry for 5 minutes.

Pour in chicken broth, salt, pepper and mix well. Cook on low heat for 25 minutes on stew mode.

Pour to serving bowls. Serve and enjoy.

126. Instant Pot Baked Whole Chicken

(Time: 70 minutes \ Servings: 6)

Ingredients:

1 while chicken

1 teaspoon garlic paste

1 teaspoon ginger paste

1 teaspoon salt

1 teaspoon cayenne pepper

¼ teaspoon chili powder

½ teaspoon black pepper

½ teaspoon cinnamon powder

½ teaspoon cumin powder

3 tablespoons lemon juice

2 tablespoons apple cider vinegar

2 tablespoons soya sauce

3 tablespoons olive oil

Directions:

In a bowl, combine vinegar, cayenne pepper, lemon juice, ginger garlic paste, salt, pepper, chili powder, olive oil, cinnamon powder, and cinnamon powder, mix well. Pour over the chicken and rub with hands all over.

Put the chicken in a greased instant pot and cover up with a lid. Let it cook on slow cook mode for 65-70 minutes. Serve and enjoy.

127. Chicken and Beans Simmer

(Time: 45 minutes \ Servings: 5)

Ingredients:

1 tablespoon olive oil

1 medium onion, chopped

4 garlic cloves, minced

1 tablespoon chopped fresh thyme

1 cup red beans, boiled

½ cup water

4 canned plum tomatoes, drained

1 can fat-free, less-sodium chicken broth

3 ounces baby spinach leaves, coarsely chopped

2 cups shredded skinless, boneless rotisserie chicken breast

½ teaspoon salt and black pepper

Directions:

Heat oil in the instant pot, add onion and stir for 2 minutes until soften. Now add the chicken, garlic and stir for another minute. Add thyme, red beans, tomatoes, salt, water and chicken broth. Cover and cook on slow medium flame on stew mode until the stew is bubbled. Add spinach and cook it for another 5 minutes. Sprinkle black pepper mix it and serve hot.

128. Hot Chicken Fingers

(Time: 40 minutes \ Servings: 8)

Ingredients:

3 chicken breasts, cut into 1 inch thick strips

1 teaspoon garlic powder

½ cup flour

½ cup bread crumbs

½ teaspoon salt

2 eggs, whisked

½ teaspoon black pepper

½ teaspoon cinnamon powder

1 cup oil, for frying

Directions:

In a platter combine flour, bread crumbs, salt, pepper, garlic powder, ad cinnamon powder, mix well. Now dip each chicken strip into the eggs then roll them out in flour mixture. Place aside. Set the instant pot on sauté mode and heat oil. Fry each chicken finger until golden and place on a paper towel. Let it drain the excessive oil. Transfer to a serving dish and serve with tomato ketchup.

129. Instant Pot Chicken Nuggets

(Time: 25 minutes \ Servings: 6)

Ingredients:

2 chicken breast, cut into small pieces

1 teaspoon garlic powder

1 teaspoon onion powder

½ cup bread crumbs

1 teaspoon salt

½ teaspoon black pepper

½ teaspoon cinnamon powder

½ teaspoon cumin powder

1 egg, whisked

1 cup oil, for frying

Directions:

In a bowl mix garlic powder, bread crumbs, onion powder, cinnamon powder, salt, pepper, and cumin powder. Now dip the chicken pieces into the whisked egg and roll out onto the bread crumbs mixture. Set the instant pot on sauté mode and heat oil well.

Deep fry each chicken nugget until nicely golden. Transfer to a paper towel.Now serve with boiled rice or any sauce. Enjoy.

130. Instant Pot Baked Chicken Breasts

(Time: 35 minutes \ Servings: 4)

Ingredients:

2 chicken breasts

2 tablespoons rice vinegar

2 tablespoons lemon juice

1 teaspoon rosemary

1 teaspoon garlic paste

1 teaspoon salt

½ teaspoon black pepper

3 tablespoons olive oil

Directions:

Combine vinegar, oil, black pepper, salt, rosemary, garlic paste, and lemon juice, mix. Drizzle over chicken and toss well. Set the instant pot on pressure cooker mode and transfer the chicken breasts in the pot. Let it cook for 35 minutes. Serve and enjoy.

131. Instant Pot Chicken Pepper Noodles

(Time: 35 minutes \ Servings: 4)

Ingredients:

¼ lb. chicken, boneless, cut into small pieces

1 package noodles, boiled

1 red bell pepper, chopped

1 green bell pepper, chopped

1 cup sour cream

1 teaspoon rosemary

2-3 garlic cloves garlic, minced

1 teaspoon salt

½ teaspoon black pepper

3 tablespoons butter

Directions:

Melt butter in the instant pot on sauté mode and fry garlic for 1 minute. Now add the chicken and stir fry until lightly golden. Season with salt and pepper. Stir in the bell peppers and sauté for 3-4 minutes. Add noodles and cream, toss well. Cook for 5-8 minutes and then turn off the flame. Transfer to a serving dish and serve hot. Enjoy.

132. Green Chicken Curry

(Time: 35 minutes \ Servings: 4)

Ingredients:

¼ lb. chicken, boneless, cut into small pieces

1 bunch green coriander

2 green chilies

2-3 garlic cloves garlic, minced

1 teaspoon salt

½ teaspoon black pepper

3 tablespoons butter

Directions:

In a blender, add coriander, green chili and tomatoes, blend until puree. Melt butter in the instant pot on sauté mode and fry garlic for 1 minute. Now add the chicken and stir fry until lightly golden.

Season with salt and pepper. Add in coriander, sauce and mix well. Let it simmer for 10-15 minutes on medium heat. Transfer to a serving dish and serve hot. Enjoy.

133. Chicken Shashlik

(Time: 35 minutes \ Servings: 4)

Ingredients:

¼ lb. chicken, boneless, cut into small pieces

2 green bell peppers, chopped

1 cup tomato ketchup

½ cup tomato sauce

1 teaspoon salt

½ teaspoon black pepper

3 tablespoons butter

Directions:

Melt butter in the instant pot on sauté mode and fry garlic for 1 minute. Now add the chicken and stir fry until lightly golden. Season with salt and pepper. Add tomato ketchup and tomato sauce, stir well. Let it simmer for 10-15 minutes on medium heat. Transfer to a serving dish and serve hot. Enjoy.

134. Broccoli Chicken

(Time: 45 minutes \ Servings: 3)

Ingredients:

¼ lb. chicken, boneless, cut into small pieces	½ teaspoon black pepper
1 cup broccoli florets	3 tablespoons butter
2-3 garlic cloves garlic, minced	1 cup chicken broth
1 teaspoon salt	2 cup cream

Directions:

Melt butter in the instant pot on sauté mode and fry garlic for 1 minute. Add the chicken and stir fry until golden. Season with salt and pepper. Add broccoli, cream, and pour in chicken broth, let it cook on manual mode for 10 minutes. Transfer to a serving dish and enjoy.

135. Instant Pot Creamy Chicken Noodles

(Time: 30 minutes \ Servings: 5)

Ingredients:

¼ lb. chicken, boneless, pieces, boiled	1 teaspoon rosemary
1 package noodles, boiled	2-3 garlic cloves garlic, minced
1 teaspoon tarragon	1 teaspoon salt
1 cup cream	½ teaspoon black pepper
¼ cup all-purpose flour	3 tablespoons butter
½ cup milk	

Directions:

Melt butter in the instant pot on sauté mode and fry garlic for 1 minute. Add in cream and flour, stir continuously. Now pour milk by continuously stirring.

Transfer the chicken and combine well.

Season with salt and pepper.

Now spread noodles into a platter and top with the creamy chicken.

Sprinkle tarragon and serve. Enjoy.

136. Instant Pot Chicken Pilaf

(Time: 45 minutes \ Servings: 5)

Ingredients:

2 cups rice, soaked
1 cup chicken, pieces
1 teaspoon cumin seeds
1 bay leaf
2 garlic cloves, minced
1 teaspoon black pepper

1 pinch turmeric powder
1 teaspoon cumin powder
2 medium onions, sliced
1 teaspoon salt
3 tablespoons olive oil
4 cups chicken broth

Directions:

Heat oil in the instant pot on sauté mode, fry onion with cumin seeds, and bay leaf until nicely golden. Now add the chicken and fry.

Season with salt, turmeric powder, pepper, garlic and fry well.

Pour in the vegetable broth and add the cumin powder, cinnamon powder, let it boil.

Add rice, let it simmer until baubles appear on top, cover the pot with a lid. Let it cook on medium heat for 20 minutes on rice mode.

Transfer to a serving dish and enjoy.

137. Instant Pot Hot Chicken Chili

(Time: 25 minutes \ Servings: 3)

Ingredients:

2 chicken breasts
1 cup chili garlic sauce
¼ cup tomato ketchup
4 tablespoons honey
2 tablespoons soya sauce

2 tomatoes, chopped
¼ teaspoon salt
¼ teaspoon cayenne pepper
3 tablespoons olive oil

Directions:

Combine the chili garlic sauce, tomato ketchup, soya sauce, honey, salt, pepper and mix. Pour sauce on the chicken and toss well. Heat oil in the instant pot on sauté mode, and transfer the chicken breasts in the pot. Cover and cook on pressure cook mode for 20 minutes. Transfer to a serving dish and serve.

138. Instant Pot Chicken Wings

(Time: 35 minutes \ Servings: 5)

Ingredients:

3 chicken breasts, cut into 2 inch pieces

1 teaspoon garlic powder

1 cup all-purpose flour

2 tablespoons coriander, chopped

½ teaspoon salt

½ teaspoon chili pepper

½ teaspoon cinnamon powder

1 cup oil, for frying

¼ cup water

Directions:

In a bowl, combine flour, salt, chili powder, cumin powder, coriander and toss well. Add water and make a thick paste. Heat oil in the instant pot on sauté mode. Dip each chicken piece into the flour mixture and then in the oil.

Fry each chicken wing until golden and place on a paper towel to drain out the excessive oil. Transfer to a serving dish and serve with mint sauce. Enjoy.

139. Instant Pot Hot Garlic Chicken Breasts

(Time: 35 minutes \ Servings: 5)

Ingredients:

2 chicken breasts
2 tablespoons apple cider vinegar
1 cup tomato ketchup
1 teaspoon garlic powder

¼ teaspoon salt
½ teaspoon chili powder
3 tablespoons olive oil

Directions:

Combine vinegar, ketchup, chili powder, salt, and garlic powder, toss well.

Drizzle over chicken and toss well. Set the instant pot on sauté mode and heat oil.

Transfer the chicken breasts in the pot. Cook for 35 minutes. Serve and enjoy.

140. Instant Pot Tropic Chicken Masala

(Time: 30 minutes \ Servings: 4)

Ingredients:

2 chicken breasts, cut into small piece
1 cup tomato ketchup
¼ cup cream
1 teaspoon garlic paste

1 teaspoon salt
½ teaspoon black pepper
2 tablespoons olive oil

Directions:

Heat oil in the instant pot on sauté mode and fry garlic for 1 minute. Now add the chicken and stir fry until lightly golden.

Season with salt and pepper.

Add ketchup and cream, let it simmer for 10 minutes on low flame.

Transfer to a serving dish and serve hot.

Enjoy.

141. Instant Pot Fried Chicken Mince

(Time: 35 minutes \ Servings: 4)

Ingredients:

1 cup ground chicken

1 onion, chopped

2-3 garlic cloves, minced

¼ teaspoon cumin powder

¼ teaspoon cinnamon powder

2 tomatoes, chopped

1 teaspoon salt

½ teaspoon black pepper

2 tablespoons olive oil

Directions:

Heat oil in the instant pot on sauté mode and fry garlic with onion for 1 minute. Add the ground chicken and stir fry until its color is changed. Season with salt and pepper.

Stir in tomatoes and sauté for 3-4 minutes. Cook for 5-8 minutes and then turn off flame.

Sprinkle cumin powder and cinnamon powder. Transfer to a serving dish and serve hot. Enjoy.

142. Chicken and Chickpea Curry

(Time: 45 minutes \ Servings: 6)

Ingredients:

1 onion, sliced

2 tomatoes, chopped

1 cup chickpea, boiled

1 cup chicken, cubes,

2 cups chicken broth

½ teaspoon garlic paste

½ teaspoon ginger paste

½ teaspoon cumin powder

½ teaspoon cinnamon power

½ teaspoon chili powder

¼ teaspoon salt

¼ teaspoon turmeric powder

3 tablespoons oil

Directions:

Heat oil in the instant pot, sauté onion for 1 minute on sauté mode. Stir in tomatoes, ginger garlic paste, salt, chili powder, turmeric powder and fry for 1 minute. Add chicken pieces, and cook until lightly golden.

Add chickpea and chicken broth and cook on low heat for 20 minutes on stew mode. Transfer to a serving dish. Sprinkle cinnamon and cumin powder. Serve and enjoy.

143. Chicken and Turnip Stew

(Time: 45 minutes \ Servings: 7)

Ingredients:

1 onion, chopped

2 tomatoes, chopped

1 cup chicken pieces

2-3 turnips, peeled, diced

2 cups chicken broth

1 carrot, sliced

1 tablespoon coriander, chopped

½ teaspoon garlic paste

½ teaspoon ginger paste

½ teaspoon cumin powder

½ teaspoon cinnamon power

½ teaspoon chili powder

¼ teaspoon salt

¼ teaspoon turmeric powder

3 tablespoons oil

2 green chilies, whole

Directions:

Heat oil, sauté onion for 1 minute on sauté mode. Stir in tomatoes, ginger garlic paste, salt, chili powder, turmeric powder and fry for 1 minute.

Now add chicken pieces, and cook until lightly golden. Add turnip and fry with chicken until it becomes tender.

Now add chicken broth, coriander, carrot, green chili, and cook on low heat for 30 minutes on stew mode. Add cinnamon and cumin powder and stir. Transfer to a serving dish and enjoy.

144. Spinach Chicken Curry

(Time: 55 minutes \ Servings: 6)

Ingredients:

1 cup chicken pieces

1 cup spinach, chopped, boiled

1 onion, chopped

2 tomatoes, chopped

2-3 turnips, peeled, diced

2 cups chicken broth

½ teaspoon garlic paste

½ teaspoon chili powder

¼ teaspoon salt

¼ teaspoon turmeric powder

3 tablespoons oil

Directions:

Heat oil in instant pot, sauté onion for 1 minute on sauté mode. Stir in tomatoes, garlic paste, salt, chili powder, turmeric powder and fry for 1 minute. Now add chicken pieces, and cook until golden.

Add spinach and fry with chicken for 5-10 minutes on high heat. Now add chicken broth, green chili, and cook on low heat for 30 minutes on stew mode. Transfer to a serving dish and enjoy.

145. Creamy Chicken Korma

(Time: 30 minutes \ Servings: 4)

Ingredients:

½ lb. chicken, boneless, pieces

1 cup cream

¼ teaspoon aniseeds, crushed

½ teaspoon garlic paste

1 teaspoon salt

½ teaspoon black pepper

3 tablespoons butter

Directions:

Melt butter in the instant pot on sauté mode and fry garlic for 1 minute. Transfer the chicken and fry until lightly golden. Season with salt and pepper. Now add the cream and mix well.

Let it simmer on low heat for 10 minutes. Sprinkle aniseeds and mix well. Transfer to serving dish and enjoy.

146. Hot Butter Chicken

(Time: 40 minutes \ Servings: 4)

Ingredients:

½ lb. chicken, boneless, pieces

1 cup tomato puree

1 inch ginger slice

1-2 red chilies

½ teaspoon garlic paste

1 teaspoon salt

¼ teaspoon black pepper

4 tablespoons butter

Directions:

In a blender, add tomato puree, chilies, ginger, garlic, salt, pepper and blend well. Melt butter in the instant pot on sauté mode and fry chicken for 5-10 minute. Transfer the tomato mixture and combine.

Now let it cook on low heat for 10-15 minutes or until the chicken is tendered. Transfer to a serving dish and enjoy.

147. Tropic Shredded Chicken

(Time: 30 minutes \ Servings: 4)

Ingredients:

3 chicken breasts, shredded, boiled

½ teaspoon garlic paste

½ teaspoon salt

½ teaspoon soya sauce

2 tablespoons barbecue sauce

½ teaspoon chili powder

2 tablespoons oil

Directions:

Heat oil in the instant pot on sauté mode and fry garlic for 1 minute. Transfer the chicken breasts and fry until lightly golden.

Add soya sauce, barbecue sauce, salt, chili powder and fry well. Place into a serving dish and enjoy.

148. Chicken and Lentils Meal

(Time: 70 minutes \ Servings: 5)

Ingredients:

2 chicken breasts, boiled, shredded

1 cup yellow lentils, soaked

1 cup split gram, soaked overnight

¼ teaspoon garlic paste

½ teaspoon salt

1 onion, sliced

1 tomato, chopped

¼ teaspoon turmeric powder

½ teaspoon chili powder

2 tablespoons oil

¼ cup olive oil, for frying

3 cups water

Directions:

Heat the oil in the instant pot on sauté mode and fry onion until nicely golden. Spread onion on paper towel and place aside. In the same pot, add lentils, water, turmeric powder and boil on presser cook mode for 30-40 minutes. Transfer the shredded chicken and boiled lentils into a blender and blend puree.

In the instant pot, add 2 tablespoons cooking oil and fry garlic for 30 seconds until lightly golden. Add tomatoes, chili powder, salt and stir fry for 5-6 minutes. Add in the chicken lentils' puree and let it simmer for 10 minutes. Serve and enjoy.

149. Instant Pot Chicken Mince and Peas

(Time: 35 minutes \ Servings: 5)

Ingredients:

1 cup chicken mince

1 cup peas

1 onion, chopped

2-3 garlic cloves, minced

¼ teaspoon cumin powder

¼ teaspoon cinnamon powder

2 tomatoes, chopped

1 teaspoon salt

½ teaspoon chili powder

2 tablespoons olive oil

1 bunch coriander, chopped

½ cup chicken broth

Directions:

Heat oil in the instant pot on sauté mode and fry garlic with onion for 1 minute.

Now add ground chicken and stir fry until its color is slightly changed. Season with salt and chili powder.

Stir in tomatoes and sauté for 3-4 minutes. Now add the peas and fry until softened. Add chicken broth on and cook on manual mode for 10-15 minutes.

Sprinkle cumin powder and cinnamon powder.

Place to a serving dish and top with coriander.

150. Instant Pot Chicken and Yellow Lentils Curry

(Time: 35 minutes \ Servings: 5)

Ingredients:

1 cup chicken mince	1 teaspoon salt
1 cup yellow lentils, boiled	½ teaspoon chili powder
2-3 garlic cloves, minced	2 tablespoons olive oil
¼ teaspoon cumin powder	1 bunch coriander, chopped
2 tomatoes, chopped	½ cup chicken broth

Directions:

Heat oil in the instant pot on sauté mode and fry garlic for 1 minute.

Now add ground chicken and stir fry until its color is slightly changed.

Season with salt and chili powder.

Stir in tomatoes and sauté for 3-4 minutes. Now add lentils and fry until softened.

Fry for10-15 minutes. Sprinkle cumin powder. Transfer to a serving dish and top with coriander.

Enjoy.

151. Instant Pot Beefalo Wings

(Time: 45 minutes \ Servings: 4)

Ingredients:

2 lean meat fillets, cut into strips

1 teaspoon garlic powder

½ cup all-purpose flour

½ teaspoon salt

½ teaspoon chili powder

½ teaspoon cinnamon powder

1 cup oil, for frying

1 egg, whisked

Directions:

In a bowl, combine flour, salt, chili powder, garlic, cumin powder, pepper, and toss. Dip each meat strip into whisked egg then roll out onto the flour mixture. Heat oil in the instant pot on sauté mode.

Transfer the meat wings into oil and fry until golden. Place on a paper towel. Let the excess oil drain out. Transfer to a serving dish and serve with any sauce. Enjoy.

152. Cabbage and Carrots with Beef

(Time: 120 minutes \ Servings: 4)

Ingredients:

2 cups cabbage shredded

½ lb. beef, small pieces

1 potato, diced

1 teaspoon salt

1 teaspoon black pepper

1 cup tomato puree

½ cup spring onion, chopped

½ teaspoon garlic paste

3 tablespoons cooking oil

5 cups vegetable broth

Directions:

In the instant pot, add all ingredients and toss well. Let it cook on low heat for 2 hours on slow cook mode. Serve and enjoy.

153. Instant Pot Meatballs

(Time: 40 minutes \ Servings: 5)

Ingredients:

2 cups ground beef

1 teaspoon garlic paste

2 tablespoons gram flour

½ teaspoon salt

½ teaspoon chili powder

½ teaspoon cinnamon powder

½ teaspoon cumin powder

1 onion, chopped

1 cup oil, for frying

Directions:

In a bowl combine beef, cinnamon powder, garlic, gram flour, salt, chili powder, cumin powder, and mix well. Make round balls and place aside. Heat oil in the instant pot on sauté mode.

Transfer the meatballs in the oil and fry until golden. Place on a paper towel. Drain out the excessive oil. Transfer to a serving dish and serve with any sauce. Enjoy.

154. Instant Pot Beef Fillets

(Time: 60 minutes \ Servings: 4)

Ingredients:

2 beef fillets

1 teaspoon garlic paste

½ teaspoons ginger paste

½ teaspoon salt

½ teaspoon chili powder

½ teaspoon cinnamon powder

½ teaspoon cumin powder

2 tablespoons papaya paste

4 tablespoons oil

Directions:

In a bowl, add all seasonings and mix well. Spread on beef fillets and rub all over.

Now place the fillets inside the instant pot and cook on pressure cook mode for 55-60 minutes. Transfer to a serving dish and serve with any sauce. Enjoy.

155. Hot Beef Curry

(Time: 60 minutes \ Servings: 4)

Ingredients:

½ lb. beef, boiled

1 cup tomato puree

1 inch ginger slice

½ teaspoon garlic paste

1 teaspoon salt

¼ teaspoon chili powder

1 cup water

½ teaspoon cumin powder

4 tablespoons oil

Directions:

Heat oil in the instant pot on sauté mode and fry tomatoes with chili powder, ginger, garlic, and salt for 5-10 minute. Add beef and fry well. Add in water and cook on stew mode for 15-20 minutes.

Sprinkle cumin powder and transfer to a serving dish. Enjoy.

156. Beef and Potato Stew

(Time: 45 minutes \ Servings: 7)

Ingredients:

1 onion, chopped

2 tomatoes, chopped

½ lb. beef, pieces, boiled

2-3 potatoes, peeled, diced

2 cups chicken broth

½ teaspoon garlic paste

½ teaspoon ginger paste

½ teaspoon cumin powder

½ teaspoon cinnamon power

½ teaspoon chili powder

¼ teaspoon salt

¼ teaspoon turmeric powder

3 tablespoons oil

2 green chilies, whole

Directions:

Heat oil in the instant pot, sauté onion for 1 minute on sauté mode. Stir in tomatoes, ginger garlic paste, salt, chili powder, turmeric powder and fry for 1 minute.

Now add the beef, and fry for 10-11 minutes.

Add potatoes and fry with the beef until slightly tendered.

Now add the chicken broth, green chili, and let it cook on low heat for 30 minutes on stew mode.

Add cinnamon and cumin powder and stir.

Transfer to a serving dish and enjoy.

157. Instant Pot Beef Rice

(Time: 45 minutes \ Servings: 5)

Ingredients:

2 cups rice, soaked

½ lb. beef, boiled, pieces

1 teaspoon cumin seeds

1 bay leaf

2 garlic cloves, minced

1 teaspoon black pepper

1 pinch turmeric powder

1 teaspoon cumin powder

2 tomatoes, chopped

2 medium onions, sliced

1 teaspoon salt

3 tablespoons olive oil

4 cups chicken broth

Directions:

Heat oil in the instant pot on sauté mode, fry onion with cumin seeds and bay leaf until nicely golden. Add tomatoes and fry well. Then add the beef and fry.

Season with salt, turmeric powder, pepper, garlic and fry well. Pour in the vegetable broth and add cumin powder, cinnamon powder, boil.

Add rice, let it simmer until baubles appear on the surface, cover the pot with a lid. Let it cook on medium heat for 20 minutes on rice mode.

Transfer to a serving dish and enjoy.

158. Beef and Split Gram Curry

(Time: 55 minutes \ Servings: 6)

Ingredients:

1 onion, sliced

2 tomatoes, chopped

1 cup split gram, boiled

½ lb. beef, boiled

2 cups chicken broth

½ teaspoon garlic paste

½ teaspoon ginger paste

½ teaspoon cumin powder

½ teaspoon cinnamon power

½ teaspoon chili powder

¼ teaspoon salt

¼ teaspoon turmeric powder

3 tablespoons oil

Directions:

Heat oil in the instant pot, sauté onion for 1 minute on sauté mode. Stir in tomatoes, ginger garlic paste, salt, chili powder, turmeric powder and fry for 1 minute. Now add the beef, and fry for 5-10 minutes. Add the split gram and stir fry for 5 minutes.

Add in chicken broth and let it cook on low heat for 20 minutes on stew mode. Transfer to a serving dish. Sprinkle cinnamon and cumin powder and enjoy.

159. Instant Pot Hot and Spicy Beef Gravy

(Time: 40 minutes \ Servings: 4)

Ingredients:

½ lb. meat, cut into small pieces, boneless

1 cup tomato puree

1 onion, chopped

1 teaspoon garlic paste1/4 teaspoon garlic paste

1 teaspoon salt

½ teaspoon chili powder

½ teaspoon cumin powder

½ teaspoon cinnamon powder

¼ teaspoon turmeric powder

2 tablespoons olive oil

Directions:

Heat oil in the instant pot on sauté mode and fry garlic with onion for a minute. Add tomato puree, salt, chili powder, turmeric powder and fry again for 4-5 minutes. Add in the boiled meat and stir fry well on high heat for 10-15 minutes. Let it cook with a few splashes of water for few minutes.

Sprinkle cumin powder, cinnamon powder and mix well. Enjoy.

160. Red Beans Tendered Beef

(Time: 120 minutes \ Servings: 4)

Ingredients:

1 can red beans

½ lb.. beef meat, pieces

2 tomatoes, slices

1 cup spring onion, chopped

1 teaspoon salt

1 teaspoon chili powder

1 teaspoon garlic powder

2 tablespoon olive oil

3 cups vegetables broth

Directions:

In the instant pot, add all ingredients and toss well. Let it cook on low heat for 2 hours on slow cook mode. Serve and enjoy.

161. Instant Pot Meat Pops

(Time: 25 minutes \ Servings: 6)

Ingredients:

1 meat fillet, cut into small pieces

1 teaspoon garlic powder

1 teaspoon onion powder

½ cup flour

¼ cup water

1 teaspoon salt

½ teaspoon black pepper

½ teaspoon cinnamon powder

½ teaspoon cumin powder

1 cup oil, for frying

Directions:

In a bowl, mix flour, water, garlic powder, bread crumbs, onion powder, cinnamon powder, salt, pepper, and cumin powder. Set the instant pot on sauté mode and heat oil well.

Now dip meat pieces into the flour mixture. Deep fry each meat pop until nicely golden. Transfer to a paper towel. Serve and enjoy.

162. Instant Pot Spicy Beef Korma

(Time: 40 minutes \ Servings: 4)

Ingredients:

½ lb. beef, boiled
½ teaspoon garlic paste
1 teaspoon salt
2 tomatoes, chopped
½ teaspoon chili powder

¼ teaspoon turmeric powder
1 cup vegetable broth
½ teaspoon cumin powder
½ teaspoon dry coriander powder
3 tablespoons oil

Directions:

Heat oil in the instant pot on sauté mode and fry garlic for 1 minute. Add tomatoes with salt, chili powder, turmeric powder and fry.

Add in the beef pieces and stir fry with a few splashes of water until the oil disappears from the sides of the pan. Let it simmer on low heat for 10 minutes. Pour in the vegetable broth and mix well.

Let it cook on slow cook mode for 30 minutes. Season with cumin powder and dry coriander powder. Transfer to a serving dish and serve. Enjoy.

163. Instant Pot Pulled Beef

(Time: 30 minutes \ Servings: 4)

Ingredients:

2 beef fillets, boiled, shredded
½ teaspoon garlic paste
½ teaspoon salt
½ teaspoon soya sauce
2 tablespoons barbecue sauce

½ cup chili garlic sauce
2 tablespoons vinegar
½ teaspoon chili powder
2 tablespoons oil

Directions:

Heat oil in the instant pot on sauté mode and fry garlic for 1 minute. Transfer the beef and fry well.

Add soya sauce, chili garlic sauce, vinegar, barbecue sauce, salt, chili powder and fry well. Transfer to a serving dish and enjoy.

164. Roasted Bell Pepper with Beef

(Time: 120 minutes \ Servings: 4)

Ingredients:

4 yellow and red bell peppers, halve, seeds

½ lb. beef, boiled

½ teaspoon garlic powder

½ teaspoon salt

½ teaspoon black pepper

3 tablespoon olive oil

Directions:

In the instant pot, add all ingredients and toss well. Let it cook on low heat for 2 hours on slow cook mode. Serve and enjoy.

165. Instant Pot Beef and Peas Gravy

(Time: 45 minutes \ Servings: 5)

Ingredients:

½ lb. beef, boiled

1 cup peas

1 onion, chopped

2-3 garlic cloves, minced

2 tomatoes, chopped

¼ teaspoon turmeric powder

¼ teaspoon cumin powder

¼ teaspoon cinnamon powder

1 teaspoon salt

½ teaspoon chili powder

2 tablespoons olive oil

½ cup chicken broth

1 green chili

Directions:

Heat oil in the instant pot on sauté mode and fry onion for 1 minute. Add in the tomatoes, chili powder, salt, turmeric powder and fry. Now add the beef and stir fry well.

Then add the peas and fry for 5-6 minutes. Add the chicken broth, green chili and place to cook on manual mode for 10-15 minutes. Sprinkle cumin powder and cinnamon powder, toss well. Transfer to a serving dish and enjoy

166. Instant Pot Cauliflower Meat

(Time: 45 minutes \ Servings: 5)

Ingredients:

½ lb. meat, boiled

1 cup cauliflower florets

1 onion, chopped

2-3 garlic cloves, minced

2 tomatoes, chopped

¼ teaspoon turmeric powder

¼ teaspoon cumin powder

¼ teaspoon cinnamon powder

1 teaspoon salt

½ teaspoon chili powder

4 tablespoons olive oil

½ cup chicken broth

1 green chili

Directions:

Heat oil on sauté mode and fry cauliflower for 3-4 minutes, place aside. In the same oil, fry onion for 1 minute. Add in tomatoes, chili powder, salt, turmeric powder and fry.

Now add the beef and stir fry well. Then add cauliflower and stir fry for 5-6 minutes. Add the chicken broth on and cook on manual mode for 10-15 minutes.

Sprinkle cumin powder and cinnamon powder, toss well.

Transfer to a serving dish.

Enjoy.

167. Instant Pot Spinach and Meat Curry

(Time: 55 minutes \ Servings: 5)

Ingredients:

½ lb. meat, boiled

1 cup spinach, chopped, boiled

1 onion, chopped

2-3 garlic cloves, minced

2 tomatoes, chopped

¼ teaspoon turmeric powder

¼ teaspoon cumin powder

¼ teaspoon cinnamon powder

1 teaspoon salt

½ teaspoon chili powder

4 tablespoons olive oil

½ cup chicken broth

1 green chili

Directions:

In a blender, add the spinach and blend until puree. Heat oil in instant pot on sauté mode and fry onion for 1 minute. Add in tomatoes, chili powder, salt, turmeric powder and fry.

Now add the beef and stir fry for 5-10 minutes on high heat. Now add to the blender the spinach and let it simmer for 5 minutes. Add the chicken broth on and cook on manual mode for 10-15 minutes.

Sprinkle cumin powder and cinnamon powder, toss well. Transfer to a serving dish. Enjoy.

168. Instant Pot Beef and Chickpea Stew

(Time: 35 minutes \ Servings: 4)

Ingredients:

½ lb. beef, boneless, pieces

1 cup chickpea, boiled

1 tomato, chopped

1 onion, chopped

1 teaspoon garlic paste

¼ teaspoon ginger paste

¼ teaspoon turmeric powder

¼ teaspoon salt

¼ teaspoon chili powder

¼ teaspoon cayenne pepper

1 carrot, sliced

¼ teaspoon cinnamon powder

½ teaspoon cumin powder

3 cups chicken broth

2 tablespoons olive oil

Directions:

Heat oil in instant pot on sauté mode and add onion and fry until transparent. Add in garlic, ginger, tomatoes, salt, cayenne pepper, chili powder, turmeric powder and fry for 4-5 minutes.

Add the beef and stir fry on high heat for 10-15 minutes with a few splashes of water. Now add the chickpea and carrot and stir fry for 5 minutes. Transfer the chicken broth, cover with a lid and cook on manual mode for 30 minutes.

Sprinkle cumin powder and cinnamon powder. Transfer to serving dish and enjoy.

169. Carrot and Beef Stew

(Time: 45 minutes \ Servings: 4)

Ingredients:

½ lb. beef, pieces

3 carrots, peeled, sliced

1 tomato, chopped

1 onion, chopped

1 teaspoon garlic paste

¼ teaspoon ginger paste

¼ teaspoon turmeric powder

¼ teaspoon salt

¼ teaspoon chili powder

¼ teaspoon cinnamon powder

½ teaspoon cumin powder

3 cups chicken broth

2 tablespoons olive oil

Directions:

Heat oil in the instant pot on sauté mode, add onion and fry until transparent. Stir in garlic, ginger, tomatoes, salt, chili powder, turmeric powder and fry for 6 minutes. Stir fry the beef for 5-6 minutes.

Now add the chickpea and stir fry for 5 minutes. Transfer the chicken broth, cover with a lid and cook on manual mode for 40 minutes.

Sprinkle cumin powder and cinnamon powder.

Transfer to a serving dish and serve.

170. Tropic Beef Pineapple Curry

(Time: 30 minutes \ Servings: 4)

Ingredients:

half lb. beef, boiled

1 cup pineapples, chunks

½ cup pineapple juice

1 teaspoon ginger paste

½ teaspoon garlic paste

1 teaspoon salt

¼ teaspoon black pepper

3 tablespoons oil

Directions:

Heat oil in the instant pot on sauté mode and fry beef with, ginger, garlic, and salt for 5-10 minute.

Stir in pineapple chunks and toss well. Season with pepper. Add in pineapple juice and let it simmer for 10-15 minutes on manual mode. Put to a serving dish and enjoy.

171. Beef with Pumpkin Bowl

(Time: 60 minutes \ Servings: 4)

Ingredients:

half lb. beef, boiled

1 cup pumpkin, peeled, chunks

½ teaspoons ginger paste

½ teaspoon garlic paste

1 teaspoon salt

1 onion, chopped

¼ teaspoon black pepper

2 cups chicken broth

3 tablespoons oil

Directions:

Heat oil in the instant pot on sauté mode and fry onion with ginger, garlic for 5-10 minute. Add the beef, pumpkin, chicken broth, salt, pepper and let it cook on slow cook mode for 50-60 minutes.

Put to serving bowls and enjoy.

172. Slow Cooked Beef Turnips

(Time: 70 minutes \ Servings: 5)

Ingredients:

half lb. beef, boiled

3 large turnips, peeled, diced

1 tomato, sliced

1 onion, sliced

1 teaspoon ginger paste

½ teaspoon garlic paste

1 teaspoon salt

¼ teaspoon chili powder

3 cups chicken broth

1 cup baby carrots

3 tablespoons oil

Directions:

In the instant pot, add all ingredients and mix well. Set on slow cook mode and cover with a lid.

Cook for 60 minutes. Serve hot and enjoy.

173. Mustard Leaves Curry with Beef

(Time: 120 minutes \ Servings: 4)

Ingredients:

3 cups mustard leaves, chopped

a fourth lb. beef

2 onions, chopped

1 teaspoon salt

2 ripe tomatoes, chopped

1 teaspoon garlic paste

½ teaspoon garlic paste

1 teaspoon red chili powder

2 green chilies whole

¼ cup tablespoons cooking oil

4 cups water

1 cup vegetable broth

Directions:

In the instant pot, add all ingredients and toss well. Let it cook on low heat for 2 hours on slow cook mode. Serve and enjoy.

174. Lentils Beef

(Time: 120 minutes \ Servings: 4)

Ingredients:

1 cup green lentils

a fourth lb. beef, pieces

1 teaspoon salt

1 teaspoon chili flakes

½ teaspoon cumin powder

2 tomatoes, chopped

½ teaspoon cinnamon powder

2 tablespoons cooking oil

3 cups vegetable broth

Directions:

In the instant pot, add all ingredients and toss well. Let it cook on low heat for 2 hours on slow cook mode. Serve and enjoy.

175. Fried Okra with Beef

(Time: 45 minutes \ Servings: 4)

Ingredients:

half lb. beef, boiled, boneless

1 cup okra, sliced

1 tomato, chopped

1 onion, sliced

1 teaspoon garlic paste

¼ teaspoon ginger paste

¼ teaspoon turmeric powder

¼ teaspoon salt

¼ teaspoon chili powder

3 cups chicken broth

¼ cup olive oil

Directions:

Heat oil on sauté mode and fry okra until nicely golden on sauté mode. Transfer to a platter and place aside. In the same pot, add onion and fry until transparent.

Stir in garlic, ginger, tomatoes, salt, chili powder, turmeric powder and fry for 6 minutes. Stir fry the beef for 5-6 minutes. Now add the fried okra and stir fry for 10-15 minutes.

Sprinkle cumin powder and cinnamon powder. Transfer to a serving dish, serve and enjoy.

176. Instant Pot Coated Mozzarella Sticks

(Time: 35 minutes \ Servings: 6)

Ingredients:

3 oz. mozzarella cheese, cut into 1 inch strips
1 teaspoon onion powder
1 cup bread crumbs
1 egg, whisked
1 teaspoon garlic powder

½ teaspoon salt
½ teaspoon chili powder
½ teaspoon cinnamon powder
1 cup oil, for frying

Directions:

In a bowl, combine bread crumbs, onion powder, salt, chili powder, garlic, cumin powder, and toss well. Dip each mozzarella stick into the whisked egg and then roll out into the bread crumbs mixture. Heat oil in the instant pot on sauté mode.

Place the sticks inside the oil and fry until nicely golden. Put them on a paper towel to drain out the excessive oil. Transfer to a serving dish and serve with any sauce. Enjoy.

177. Instant Pot Potato Chips

(Time: 30 minutes \ Servings: 4)

Ingredients:

3 potatoes, sliced
¼ teaspoon salt
1 teaspoon thyme
¼ teaspoon black pepper

¼ garlic powder
2 tablespoons lemon juice
½ cup cooking oil, for frying

Directions:

Heat oil in the instant pot on sauté mode. Fry some chips until nicely golden and crispy. Transfer to a paper towel and drain out excessive oil. Season with thyme, garlic powder, salt and pepper.

Drizzle lemon juice and enjoy.

178. Fried Mushrooms

(Time: 15 minutes \ Servings: 4)

Ingredients:

2 oz. mushrooms, sliced

¼ teaspoon salt

¼ teaspoon black pepper

¼ garlic powder

4 tablespoons oil, for frying

Directions:

Heat oil the in instant pot on sauté mode. Fry mushrooms until nicely golden. Transfer to a paper towel and let the oil drain out. Season with garlic powder, salt and pepper. Drizzle lemon juice and enjoy.

179. Spiced Carrots

(Time: 55 minutes \ Servings: 3)

Ingredients:

2 oz. carrots, sliced

¼ teaspoon salt

¼ teaspoon black pepper

2 tablespoons lemon juice

1 cup orange juice

2 tablespoons oil, for frying

Directions:

Heat oil the in instant pot on sauté mode.

Add carrots and let it simmer for 10-15 minutes.

Season with salt and pepper. Add in orange juice. Cover and cook on slow cook mode for 35 minutes.

Drizzle lemon juice on top.

Serve.

180. Fried Shrimps

(Time: 25 minutes \ Servings: 3)

Ingredients:

2 oz. carrots, sliced

¼ teaspoon salt

¼ teaspoon black pepper

2 tablespoons lemon juice

1 teaspoon garlic powder

2 tablespoons oil, for frying

Directions:

Heat oil in the instant pot on sauté mode. Add shrimps and stir fry for 10-15 minutes. Season with salt, garlic and pepper. Fry for another 10 minutes. Drizzle lemon juice and toss well. Serve and enjoy.

181. Stir Fried Cherry Tomatoes

(Time: 15 minutes \ Servings: 4)

Ingredients:

2 cups cherry tomatoes

¼ teaspoon salt

¼ teaspoon black pepper

3 tablespoons vinegar

2 tablespoons oil, for frying

Directions:

Heat oil in the instant pot on sauté mode. Add shrimps and stir fry for 10-15 minutes.

Season with salt and pepper.

Now add vinegar and toss. Stir fry for 4 minutes.

Serve and enjoy.

182. Easy Rice Smash with Potatoes

(Time: 60 minutes \ Servings: 4)

Ingredients:

1 cup rice, soaked

2 potatoes, peeled, diced

1 pinch salt

¼ teaspoon black pepper

2 cups of water

2 tablespoons olive oil

1 onion, chopped

2 garlic cloves, minced

Directions:

Transfer all ingredients into the instant pot and set it to slow cook mode. Let it prepare for 55 minutes. Now let it cool and then mash with a potato masher. Put to a serving dish and serve.

183. Instant Pot Potato Wings

(Time: 35 minutes \ Servings: 6)

Ingredients:

3 large potatoes, cut into wings

2 tablespoons gram flour

1 teaspoon garlic powder

½ teaspoon salt

½ teaspoon black pepper

½ teaspoon cinnamon powder

½ teaspoon cumin powder

2 tablespoons lemon juice

1 cup oil, for frying

Directions:

In a bowl, combine flour, salt, garlic, pepper, cumin powder, cinnamon powder and toss. Add in the potato wings and toss. Heat oil in the instant pot on sauté mode.

Transfer the potatoes into the oil and fry until nicely golden. Place on a paper towel and the oil drain out.

Transfer to a serving dish, drizzle some lemon juice on top and serve.

184. Instant Pot Crispy Okra

(Time: 25 minutes \ Servings: 6)

Ingredients:

2 oz. okra, heads removed

½ teaspoon salt

½ teaspoon black pepper

¼ cup oil, for frying

Directions:

Slice the okra lengthwise. Heat oil in the instant pot on sauté mode. Transfer the okra into the oil and fry until nicely golden. Place on a paper towel so excessive oil drains out.

Season with salt and pepper. Transfer to a serving dish and enjoy.

185. Fried Pumpkin

(Time: 25 minutes \ Servings: 4)

Ingredients:

1 cup pumpkin, chunks

½ teaspoon salt

½ teaspoon black pepper

¼ teaspoon chili powder

2 tablespoons gram flour

¼ cup oil, for frying

Directions:

Combine flour, chili powder, salt, pepper and toss. Add pumpkin and mix well. Heat oil in the instant pot on sauté mode.

Transfer the pumpkin chunks into the oil and fry until nicely golden.

Place on a paper towel let the oil drain out. Season with salt and pepper.

Transfer to a serving dish and enjoy.

186. Crunchy Garlic Bread

(Time: 20 minutes \ Servings: 6)

Ingredients:

1 French baguette

3garlic cloves, minced

2 tablespoons oil

½ teaspoon salt

½ teaspoon black pepper, freshly ground

Directions:

With the help of sharp knife, cut baguette to make 8 slices. Mix olive oil, garlic, black pepper, and salt in a bowl. Brush this mixture onto each bread slice and transfer into baking sheet.

Now put this sheet into the instant pot and let it cook for 15 minutes on pressure cook mode.

187. Crispy Chicken Fritters

(Time: 25 minutes \ Servings: 4)

Ingredients:

6 chicken breast's fillets

½ cup bread crumbs

1 teaspoon garlic powder

1 teaspoon onion powder

1 teaspoon dry coriander powder

1 teaspoon cumin powder

Oil spray

1 egg

1 teaspoon salt

½ teaspoon black pepper

Directions:

In a bowl, mix breadcrumbs with coriander powder, onion powder, cumin powder, salt, black pepper and toss well. Roll each chicken fillet into the breadcrumb's mixture and transfer into a platter.

Place chicken fillets into the instant pot and set it on pressure cook mode.

Let it prepare for 20 minutes. Serve with tomato ketchup and enjoy.

188. Sweet Potato Wedges

(Time: 25 minutes \ Servings: 4)

Ingredients:

3 medium sweet potatoes, cut into wedges

1 teaspoon garlic powder

½ teaspoon salt

½ teaspoon black pepper

½ teaspoon cinnamon powder

½ teaspoon cumin powder

2 tablespoons lemon juice

1 cup oil, for frying

Directions:

In a bowl, combine salt, garlic, pepper, cumin powder, cinnamon powder and toss. Place aside.

Heat oil in the instant pot on sauté mode. Transfer the sweet potato into the oil and fry until nicely golden. Place on a paper towel. Let it drain out the excessive oil. Season with salt and pepper mixture. Transfer to a serving dish, drizzle some lemon juice on top and serve.

189. Instant Pot Spiced Fried Cauliflower

(Time: 35 minutes \ Servings: 2)

Ingredients:

1 cup cauliflower florets

1 teaspoon onion powder

1 cup all-purpose flour

1 teaspoon garlic powder

½ teaspoon salt

½ teaspoon chili powder

½ teaspoon cinnamon powder

1 cup oil, for frying

Directions:

In a bowl, combine flour, onion powder, salt, chili powder, garlic, cumin powder, and toss. Add in cauliflower and mix well. Heat oil in instant pot on sauté mode.

Transfer cauliflower into oil and fry till nicely golden. Place on paper towel. Let to drain out excess oil. Transfer to serving dish and serve with any sauce.

190. Instant Pot Spiced Chickpea

(Time: 15 minutes \ Servings: 3)

Ingredients:

1 cup chickpeas, boiled

½ teaspoon salt

½ teaspoon black pepper

¼ teaspoon cayenne pepper

2 tablespoons tamarind pulp

1 tablespoons vinegar

¼ cup oil, for frying

Directions:

Heat oil in the instant pot on sauté mode. Fry chickpeas until lightly golden brown.

Drain out the excessive oil and a paper towel.Transfer to a serving dish season with salt, pepper, tamarind pulp, cayenne pepper and mix well. Drizzle vinegar on top and enjoy.

191. Instant Pot Salty Fried Peanuts

(Time: 10 minutes \ Servings: 4)

Ingredients:

2 cups peanuts

1 bay leaf

¼ cup oil, for frying

Directions:

Heat oil in the instant pot on sauté mode. Fry the bay leaf for 20 seconds and discard it.

In same oil add peanuts and fry well. Place to a paper towel and let the excessive oil to drain out.

Sprinkle salt and toss to combine.

Enjoy.

192. Instant Pot Roasted Nuts

(Time: 10 minutes \ Servings: 12)

Ingredients:

1 cup almonds

1 cup pistachios

1 cup pine nuts

½ cup walnuts

½ cup peanuts

¼ cup oil, for frying

Directions:

Heat oil in the instant pot on sauté mode. Fry the bay leaf for 20 seconds and discard it.

In same oil add peanuts and fry well. Place to a paper towel and let the excessive oil to drain out.

Sprinkle salt and toss to combine. Enjoy.

193. Instant Pot Bruschetta with Potato Smash

(Time: 10 minutes \ Servings: 4)

Ingredients:

1 cup potatoes

2 tablespoons lemon juice

1 pinch salt

¼ teaspoon black pepper

2 cups of water

1 French bread

Directions:

Transfer the potatoes into the instant pot with water and let it boil. Now let it cool and then mash with a potato masher. Season with salt and pepper.

Cut the french bread into slices, top each slice with mashed potatoes.

Place into a serving dish and drizzle lemon juice, enjoy.

194. Instant Pot Creamy Mashed Potatoes

(Time: 30 minutes \ Servings: 3)

Ingredients:

4 large potatoes, boiled peeled

1 cup sour cream

½ cup heavy cream

1 pinch salt

¼ teaspoon black pepper

Directions:

Place the boiled potatoes, sour cream, heavy cream into the instant pot and cover with a lid. Let it cook on slow cook mode for 30 minutes. Season with salt and pepper. Serve and enjoy.

195. Instant Pot Chickpea Hummus

(Time: 60 minutes \ Servings: 4)

Ingredients:

1 cup chickpea, soaked

1 pinch salt

¼ teaspoon chili powder

3 cups of water

2 tablespoons olive oil

2 garlic cloves, minced

Directions:

Transfer the water, chickpea, salt, and garlic into the instant pot. Set it on pressure cook mode.

Cover with a lid and cook for 55 minutes. Now let it cool a little, then transfer the boiled chickpea into a blender and blend until puree.

Add olive oil gradually and blend. Put to a serving dish and sprinkle chili powder on top.

196. Instant Pot Zucchini and Potato Hummus

(Time: 40 minutes \ Servings: 4)

Ingredients:

4 large zucchini

2 potatoes, boiled, mashed

1 pinch salt

¼ teaspoon black pepper

2 cups chicken broth

2 tablespoons olive oil

2 garlic cloves, minced

Directions:

Transfer the chicken broth, zucchini, potatoes, salt, and garlic into the instant pot. Set it on slow cook mode and let it cook for 35 minutes. Now let it cool for a while and then transfer it to a blender until puree.

Add olive oil gradually and blend again. Put to a serving dish and sprinkle pepper on top.

197. Easy Cauliflower Hummus

(Time: 50 minutes \ Servings: 4)

Ingredients:

2 cups cauliflower, chunks

1 pinch salt

¼ teaspoon chili powder

3 cups of water

2 tablespoons olive oil

1 onion, chopped

2 garlic cloves, minced

Directions:

Transfer the water, cauliflower, salt, onion and garlic into the instant pot. Set it on slow cook mode.

Cover with a lid and cook for 45 minutes. Now let it cool a little then transfer into blender and blend until puree. Add olive oil gradually and blend.

Put to a serving dish and sprinkle chili powder on top. Enjoy.

198. Instant Pot Chicken Bites

(Time: 55 minutes \ Servings: 6)

Ingredients:

2 chicken breast

4 tablespoons breadcrumbs

½ teaspoon salt

1 egg

1 teaspoon black pepper

1 teaspoon red paprika

1 bunch of parsley

2 tablespoons oil

Directions:

With a sharp knife cut the chicken breasts into small chunks. In a bowl, put the chicken breasts; sprinkle salt, black pepper, 1 egg, and breadcrumbs. Add oil in the instant pot and transfer the chicken into it.

Set the pot on slow cook mode. Let it cook on medium heat for 50 minutes. Serve and enjoy.

199. Stir Fried Spinach

(Time: 20 minutes \ Servings: 3)

Ingredients:

1 bunch baby spinach leaves

½ teaspoon salt

1 teaspoon black pepper

2 garlic cloves, minced

2 tablespoons soya sauce

1 teaspoon lemon juice

2 tablespoons oil

Directions:

Heat oil in the instant pot and stir fry garlic for 1 minute on sauté mode. Add spinach and sauté for 10-15 minutes. Now season it with salt, pepper, soya sauce, and lemon juice. Serve and enjoy.

200. Ginger Zest Pineapple Slices

(Time: 15 minutes \ Servings: 3)

Ingredients:

2 cups pineapple slices

1 pinch salt

¼ teaspoon black pepper

1 inch ginger slice, chopped

1 teaspoon lemon juice

2 tablespoons oil

Directions:

Heat oil in the instant pot and stir fry ginger for 1 minute on sauté mode.

Add in pineapple and stir fry well.

Season with salt, and pepper.

Drizzle lemon juice and toss well.

Serve and enjoy..

201. Instant Pot Carrot and Rice Pudding

(Time: 55 minutes \ Servings: 6)

Ingredients:

6 carrots, shredded

1 cup pineapple, chunks

1 cup rice, boiled

½ cup sugar

1 cup raisins

2 green cardamoms

5-6 pistachio, chopped

2 cups milk

1 cup water

1 pinch of salt

Directions:

In the instant pot, transfer the boiled rice, shredded carrots, pineapple, sugar, milk, salt, and cardamom, and cover with a lid. Let it to cook on slow cook mode for 60 minutes.

Place pudding into the freezer for 15 minutes and top with pistachios.

202. Strawberry Cake

(Time: 50 minutes \ Servings: 4)

Ingredients:

2 cups all-purpose flour

1 cup fresh strawberries

2 cup strawberry puree

1 teaspoon baking powder

1 cup butter

1 pinch salt

2 eggs

1 cup milk

1 cup sugar

1 cup whipped cream

2 tablespoons caster sugar

1 teaspoon vanilla extract

Directions:

In the instant pot place a trivet and add 2-3 cups of water in the pot.

In a bowl, add flour, eggs, sugar, salt, baking powder, milk, butter, vanilla extract and beat well.

Add the strawberry puree and stir. Pour into a greased cake pan and place on a trivet.

Let it prepare for 40 minutes on pressure cook mode.

Toss the caster sugar with the whipped cream to mix well. When the cake is cooled, top it with the whipped cream and place the strawberries.

Serve and enjoy.

203. Lemon Cake

(Time: 50 minutes \ Servings: 6)

Ingredients:

2 cups all-purpose flour	1 pinch salt
2 tablespoons lemon zest	4 eggs
2 tablespoons lemon juice	1 cup coconut milk
1 teaspoon baking powder	1 cup sugar
¼ teaspoon baking soda	½ cup honey
½ cup butter	½ cup apple jam

Directions:

In the instant pot, place a stand or a trivet and add 2 cups of water. Combine the flour, sugar, salt, baking powder, baking soda, eggs, lemon juice butter, milk, 1 tablespoon lemon zest and beat with electric beater.

Transfer to a greased baking pan and place on a trivet, cover and cook on pressure cook mode for 30-40 minutes. Combine the apple jam with honey.

Pour this mixture onto the cake and top with lemon zest. Serve and enjoy.

204. Chocolate Crackers

(Time: 40 minutes \ Servings: 6)

Ingredients:

1 cups all-purpose flour

1 cup cocoa powder

½ cup molten chocolate

½ teaspoon baking powder

½ cup butter

2 eggs

1 cup caster sugar

Directions:

Grease the instant pot with cooking spray. Combine all ingredients in a bowl and knead a soft dough. Roll out the dough on a clean surface. Cut with a cookie cutter.

Place into the greased instant pot and prepare for 30 minutes on manual mode. Serve and enjoy.

205. Chocolate Pudding

(Time: 50 minutes \ Servings: 6)

Ingredients:

1 cup milk

1 cup chocolate, melted

4 bananas, peeled, sliced

½ cup condense milk

½ cup sugar

2 tablespoons butter

2 tablespoons cocoa powder

1 cup whipped cream

Directions:

In the instant pot, add the butter and the whipped cream and let it cook until reduced to half. Now add the condensed milk, chocolate, sugar, cocoa powder and stir gradually.

Pour half of the chocolate pudding into a large dish and place the banana slices evenly. Pour the remaining chocolate on top and freeze for 2 hours.

206. Instant Pot Pumpkin and Pineapple Cobbler

(Time: 50 minutes \ Servings: 4)

Ingredients:

1 cup ripe pumpkin, peeled, chunks

1 cup pineapple, chunks

1 cup milk

½ cup sugar

1 teaspoon pumpkin pie spice

1 cup whipped cream for toping

Directions:

In the instant pot, add pumpkin, pineapples, milk, sugar, pumpkin pie spice and cover. Let it cook on slow cook mode for 50 minutes. Put to serving dish and top with whipped cream.

207. Velvet Chocolate Pudding

(Time: 40 minutes \ Servings: 4)

Ingredients:

1 cup raw chocolate, melted

1 teaspoon vanilla extract

1 cup cocoa powder

2 tablespoons butter

¼ cup caster sugar

½ cup chocolate syrup

2 cups milk

2 eggs

½ cup chocolate chips

Directions:

Beat eggs until fluffy. In the instant pot, add butter and milk, let it boil. Now add the cocoa powder and stir continuously. Add caster sugar and eggs by stirring gradually.

Now transfer the melted chocolate in it mix thoroughly. Transfer into a serving dish and place inside the freezer for 20 minutes.

Drizzle chocolate syrup on top. Serve and enjoy.

208. Mango and Sweet Potato Smash

(Time: 50 minutes \ Servings: 4)

Ingredients:

1 cup mango cubes

½ cup sugar

3 sweet potatoes, peeled, cubes

1 cup milk

1 cup cream

½ cup water

Directions:

In the instant pot add mangoes, sugar, milk, cream, sweet potatoes and water, cover with a lid. Let it cook for 50 minutes on slow cook mode on very low heat.

Now transfer this mixture into a bowl, mash it slightly with fork and sprinkle some black pepper if you like. Enjoy.

209. Chocolate Silk Bowls

(Time: 35 minutes \ Servings: 4)

Ingredients:

2 cups raw chocolate

¼ cup cocoa powder

2 tablespoons brown sugar

1 cup milk

¼ cup heavy cream

3 tablespoons butter

Directions:

Melt the butter in on sauté mode.

Add milk, brown sugar, chocolate, cream, and cook well on slow cook mode for 30 minutes. Stir occasionally.

Place to small serving bowls and place inside the fridge for 10 minutes. Serve and enjoy.

210. Pineapple and Mango Blossom

(Time: 50 minutes \ Servings: 3)

Ingredients:

1 cup mango, chunks

1 cup pineapple slices

1 cup milk

½ cup sugar

½ teaspoons vanilla extract

1 cup whipped cream

½ cup pomegranates

Directions:

In the instant pot, add milk, pineapple, sugar and mangoes cover with a lid, cook for about 50 minutes on slow cook mode.

Transfer to a serving dish when cooled, add 2-3 spoons of whipped cream on top and sprinkle pomegranates as much you like.

211. Cinnamon Spiced Apples

(Time: 20 minutes \ Servings: 3)

Ingredients:

1 cup apple, peeled and diced

1 cup milk

½ cup sugar

½ teaspoon cinnamon powder

¼ teaspoon black pepper

4 tablespoons honey

1 pinch salt

Directions:

In a large bowl, toss apples, cinnamon powder, black pepper, salt and transfer into the instant pot.

Stir in milk, sugar and cover with a lid. Let it cook for 35 minutes on slow cook mode.

Put to a serving dish and drizzle honey on top. Serve and enjoy.

212. Sweet and Sour Pears

(Time: 25 minutes \ Servings: 3)

Ingredients:

3 pears, sliced

¼ cup brown sugar

4 tablespoons maple syrup

1 tablespoons lemon juice

1 pinch salt

3 tablespoons butter

Directions:

Melt butter inside the instant pot and add pears, stir fry for 10 to 15 minutes on sauté mode. Add brown sugar and salt, dissolve it. Stir continuously.

Transfer to a serving dish and top with maple syrup. Drizzle lemon juice. Serve and enjoy.

213. Instant Pot Blackberry Smash

(Time: 40 minutes \ Servings: 4)

Ingredients:

1 cup black berries

2 tablespoons all-purpose flour

1 cup milk

1 cup cream

½ cup sugar

2 tablespoons butter

Directions:

In the instant pot, melt butter on sauté mode.

Add flour and stir well. Pour in the milk and stir continuously.

Add in the cream, blackberries, sugar, and prepare on slow cook mode for 30 minutes.

Serve and enjoy.

214. Instant Pot Mouth-melting Bread Pudding

(Time: 60 minutes \ Servings: 4)

Ingredients:

6 slices of bread, roughly shredded

4 eggs

½ cup sugar

½ teaspoon cardamom powder

¼ teaspoon vanilla extract

1 cup milk

1 cup mozzarella cheese, shredded

1 pinch salt

1 tablespoon butter

Directions:

In a large bowl, beat eggs with a pinch of salt for 3-4 minutes. Transfer to the instant pot, add the bread slices, milk, cardamom powder, butter, cheese, sugar, vanilla extract and cook for 60 minutes on slow cook mode on low heat. Serve hot.

215. Instant Pot Pistachio Cake

(Time: 50 minutes \ Servings: 4)

Ingredients:

2 tbsp. pistachio powder

4-5 tablespoons mint leaves, finely chopped

½ cup sugar

1 cup all-purpose flour

1 teaspoon vanilla extract

1 tablespoon cocoa powder

2 eggs

½ cup butter

Directions:

In a large bowl, beat eggs until fluffy. Now in another bowl, beat the butter with sugar, add vanilla extract and beat for 1-2 minutes. Now add it to the eggs mixture and fold flour, vanilla extract, mint leaves, pistachio powder. Pour the butter into the greased instant pot and cover with a lid.

Cook on pressure cook mode for 45 minutes. Sever and enjoy.

216. Banana and Strawberry Pudding

(Time: 40 minutes \ Servings: 3)

Ingredients:

1 cup banana, slices

1 cub strawberries

2 cups milk

½ cup sugar

3 tablespoons honey

½ teaspoon cardamom powder

Directions:

In the instant pot, add milk, banana, strawberries, sugar, and cardamom powder, cover with a lid.

Let it cook to for 40 minutes on slow cook mode.

Transfer to a dish and top with honey and enjoy.

217. Cardamom Zest Banana Pudding

(Time: 20 minutes \ Servings: 3)

Ingredients:

4 ripe bananas, mashed

2 cups milk

½ cup sugar

2 green cardamoms

Directions:

In the instant pot, add milk and boil on pressure cook mode.

Now add sugar and stir well.

Add the mashed bananas, cardamom and stir for 5-10 minutes.

Transfer to a dish and enjoy.

218. Carrot and Honey Pie

(Time: 60 minutes \ Servings: 3)

Ingredients:

1 cup shredded carrot

1 cups of milk

1 cup shredded mozzarella cheese

½ cup condense milk

1 teaspoon cardamom powder

4-5 almonds, chopped

4-5 pistachios, chopped

¼ cup sugar

Directions:

In the instant pot, place carrots, milk, condense milk, mozzarella cheese, cardamom powder, sugar and cover. Cook for 60 minutes on slow cook mode.

Transfer into a serving dish and top with chopped pistachios and almonds.

219. Rice Pudding with Chocolate Chips

(Time: 50 minutes \ Servings: 4)

Ingredients:

1 cup mango, chopped

1 cup rice, boiled

2 cups of milk

½ cup sugar

½ cup chocolate chips

2 tablespoons honey

1 pinch salt

Directions:

In the instant pot, add mangoes, rice, milk, sugar, chocolate chips and pinch of salt, and cook on low heat for 2 hour, stir occasionally. Serve with honey on top.

220. Cherry Delight

(Time: 40 minutes \ Servings: 3)

Ingredients:

1 cup fresh cherries, chopped

½ cup pomegranates

2 cup milk

1 cup whipped cream

½ cup sugar

1 tsp. vanilla extract

1 pinch of salt

½ cup pineapple slices

Directions:

In the instant pot, add cherries, milk, sugar, vanilla extract and salt, cover with a lid. Cook on low heat for 40 minutes. Serve with pomegranate, whipped cream and pineapples slices on top.

221. Coconut Peach Crumble

(Time: 30 minutes \ Servings: 3)

Ingredients:

1 cup peach chunks

1 cup milk

½ cup sugar

1 pinch of salt

½ cup coconut powder

1 tbsp. almond powder

½ tsp. cardamom powder

½ cup Pineapple slices

Directions:

In the instant pot, add peaches, milk, sugar, coconut powder, almond powder, cardamom powder, and salt. Cook on stew mode for 30 minutes.

Stir occasionally.

Serve with pineapple slices on top..

222. Cheese Fruit Smash

(Time: 40 minutes \ Servings: 4)

Ingredients:

1 cup mango chunks

1 cup banana chunks

1 cup peach chunks

1 cup strawberry chunks

1 cup blueberry chopped

½ cup pomegranate

1 cup whipped cream

1 cup cherries, chopped

¼ cup sugar

1 cup coconut milk

1 cup mozzarella cheese, shredded

Directions:

In the instant pot, add pineapples, mangoes, bananas, cheese, sugar, coconut milk, strawberries and blueberries, cover with a lid. Cook for 40 minutes on slow cook mode.

Serve with pomegranates and whipped cream on top. Enjoy.

223. Coconut Milk Apple Crumble

(Time: 40 minutes \ Servings: 4)

Ingredients:

1 cup apple, diced

1 cup coconut milk

½ cup sugar

1 banana, chopped

1 tsp. cardamom powder

3-4 almonds, crushed

Directions:

In the instant pot add apples, coconut milk, cardamom powder, banana and sugar, cook it on slow cook mode for 40 minutes.

When apples are tender, smash with fork and transfer to a serving dish. Sprinkle almonds on top.

Enjoy.

224. Bloody Plum Pudding

(Time: 50 minutes \ Servings: 5)

Ingredients:

1 cup ripe plums

½ cup sugar

2 cups of water

1 tbsp. sesame seeds

1 pinch of salt

Directions:

In the instant pot, add whole plums, sugar, water, sesame seeds and pinch of salt. Let it cook for 40 minutes on slow cook mode. Discard seeds of plums if you like. Enjoy.

225. Strawberry Sauce

(Time: 40 minutes \ Servings: 3)

Ingredients:

2 cups strawberries

1 cup pineapple juice

½ cup sugar

1 pinch of salt

Directions:

In the instant pot, add all ingredients and cover with a lid.

Set the pot on slow cook mode and cook for 40 minutes.

Transfer to a serving dish and serve.

Enjoy.

226. Instant Pot Egg and Onion Frittata

(Time: 25 minutes \ Servings: 3)

Ingredients:

4 eggs, whisked

1 onion, chopped

1 green chili, chopped

¼ teaspoons slat

½ teaspoon black pepper

3 tablespoons butter

Directions:

In a bowl, add eggs, onion, green chilies, salt, and pepper, mix well. Melt butter in the instant pot on sauté mode. Transfer the eggs mixture and spread all over.

Let it cook for 2-3 minutes from one side then flip to the other. Cook for 1-2 minutes and then transfer to a serving platter. Serve hot and enjoy.

227. Instant Pot Egg and Carrot Spread

(Time: 25 minutes \ Servings: 3)

Ingredients:

4 eggs, whisked

3 carrots, shredded, boiled

¼ teaspoons slat

½ teaspoon black pepper

3 tablespoons butter

Directions:

In a blender, add the carrots and blend them until puree. Add them to the instant pot and let simmer for 2 minutes. Add the eggs, butter, salt and pepper, stir continually for 10-15 minutes.

Cook for 5 minutes on low heat. Serve hot and enjoy.

228. Instant Pot Egg Scramble

(Time: 10 minutes \ Servings: 3)

Ingredients:

4 eggs

1 pinch of salt

½ teaspoon black pepper

1 cup milk

3 tablespoons butter

Directions:

Melt butter in the pot on sauté mode. Crack the eggs in the pot and add milk, stir continuously for 5 minutes.

Transfer to a serving platter and scramble again with a fork for a minute. Serve and enjoy.

229. Instant Pot Egg Salad with Carrots

(Time: 15 minutes \ Servings: 3)

Ingredients:

4 eggs

1 carrot, sliced

1 potato, boiled, diced

1 green chili, chopped

1 pinch of salt

½ teaspoon black pepper

1 cup cream

3 tablespoons butter

Directions:

Melt butter in the instant pot on sauté mode. Crack eggs in the pot and add milk, stir continuously for 5 minutes.

Transfer to a serving platter and scramble again with a fork for 1 minute. Now combine with the cream, chilies, potatoes, carrots, and toss well.

Serve and enjoy.

230. Instant Pot Egg and Carrots Crum

(Time: 25 minutes \ Servings: 3)

Ingredients:

4 eggs

1 carrot, shredded

1 pinch of salt

½ teaspoon black pepper

3 tablespoons butter

Directions:

Melt butter in the pot on sauté mode.

Sauté carrots for 5-10 minutes until water of carrots is dried out. Add the eggs, salt and pepper, stir continuously. Cook for 5 minutes. Enjoy.

231. Half Fry Eggs

(Time: 5 minutes \ Servings: 2)

Ingredients:

2 eggs

1 pinch of salt

½ teaspoon black pepper

3 tablespoons oil

Directions:

Heat oil in the instant pot on sauté mode.

Crack eggs in the pot and cook for 2-3 minutes.

Transfer to a platter and season with salt and pepper.

Serve and enjoy.

232. Bell Peeper and Egg Frittata

(Time: 25 minutes \ Servings: 3)

Ingredients:

4 eggs, whisked

1 red bell pepper, chopped

1 onion, chopped

¼ teaspoons slat

½ teaspoon black pepper

3 tablespoons butter

Directions:

In a bowl, add the eggs, onion, bell peppers, salt, and pepper, mix well.

Melt butter in the pot on sauté mode.

Pour the eggs mixture and spread all over and cover the pot with a lid.

Cook for 15 minutes on manual mode. Serve hot and enjoy.

233. Instant Pot Hard Boiled Eggs

(Time: 20 minutes \ Servings: 4)

Ingredients:

4 eggs

2 tablespoons salt

3 cups water

Directions:

Fill the instant pot with water and add salt. Place the eggs in the water carefully and cover up with a lid.

Let them boil on stew mode for 20 minutes. Remove from the pot and place to cold water.

Serve and enjoy.

234. Eggs Filled Avocado

(Time: 20 minutes \ Servings: 2)

Ingredients:

2 eggs

1 avocado, pitted, halved

1 pinch salt

1 pinch black pepper

2 tablespoons olive oil

Directions:

Spray the instant pot with oil. Place the avocados in the instant pot and crack eggs into each avocado hole. Sprinkle salt and pepper.

Cover with a lid and cook for 15 minutes on pressure cook mode. Serve and enjoy.

235. Roasted Eggs Gravy

(Time: 30 minutes \ Servings: 4)

Ingredients:

4 eggs, hard boiled, peeled

1 onion, chopped

2 tomatoes, chopped

¼ teaspoon pinch salt

½ teaspoon chili powder

¼ teaspoon turmeric powder

1/3 teaspoon cumin powder

1-2 garlic cloves, minced

2 tablespoons olive oil

Directions:

Heat oil in the instant pot on sauté mode and fry eggs until lightly golden. Place aside.

In the same oil, fry onion until lightly golden. Add tomatoes, garlic, salt, chili powder, turmeric powder and fry until the tomatoes are softened. Now transfer into a blender and blend well.

Return to the pot again and fry with a few splashes of water. Add the roasted eggs and toss well. Transfer to a serving platter and enjoy.

236. Squash with Eggs

(Time: 30 minutes \ Servings: 4)

Ingredients:

4 eggs

1 squash, cut into 1 inch thick rings

1 pinch salt

1 pinch chili powder

2 tablespoons olive oil

Directions:

Spray the instant pot with oil. Place the squash rings in the instant pot and crack an egg into each ring. Sprinkle salt and pepper.

Cover with a lid and cook for 25 minutes on pressure cook mode. Serve and enjoy

237. Instant Pot Eggs Curry

(Time: 25 minutes \ Servings: 5)

Ingredients:

4 eggs, hard boiled, sliced

1 onion, chopped

2 tomatoes, chopped

¼ teaspoon pinch salt

½ teaspoon chili powder

¼ teaspoon turmeric powder

1/3 teaspoon cumin powder

1-2 garlic cloves, minced

2 tablespoons olive oil

Directions:

Heat oil in the instant pot on sauté mode and fry onion for 1 minute. Add tomatoes, garlic, salt, chili powder, turmeric powder and fry until the tomatoes are softened. Now transfer this gravy into a blender and blend well. Return to the pot again and fry with a few splashes of water.

Add egg slices and combine. Transfer to a serving platter and enjoy.

238. Breads Chunks with Eggs

(Time: 10 minutes \ Servings: 3)

Ingredients:

3 bread slices

3 eggs

1 pinch salt

2 tablespoons olive oil

Directions:

Place a cutter at the center of the bread and cut it to make a round hole. Repeat same for all bread slices. Spray the instant pot with oil. Place the bread slices inside and crack the eggs in.

Repeat for all slices. Sprinkle salt. Cover with a lid and cook for 5 minutes on pressure cook mode.

Serve and enjoy.

239. Traditional Egg Bahaji

(Time: 20 minutes \ Servings: 3)

Ingredients:

2 eggs, whisked

1 onion, chopped

2 tomatoes, chopped

½ teaspoons chili powder

¼ teaspoon salt

2 tablespoons olive oil

Directions:

Heat oil in the instant pot on sauté mode, fry onion until transparent. Now add the tomatoes and stir fry well. Season with salt and pepper.

Pour the whisked eggs and stir consciously for 2 minutes.

Transfer to a serving platter, serve and enjoy.

240. Instant Pot Cheese Omelette

(Time: 15 minutes \ Servings: 2)

Ingredients:

2 eggs, whisked

1 teaspoon garlic powder

¼ teaspoons slat

½ teaspoon black pepper

½ cup parmesan cheese, shredded

½ cup mozzarella cheese, shredded

3 tablespoons butter

Directions:

In a bowl, add the eggs, mozzarella and parmesan cheese, season with salt, garlic, and pepper. Melt butter in the instant pot on sauté mode. Pour the eggs' mixture and spread evenly all over.

Let it cook for 2-3 minutes from one side then flip. Cook for 1-2 minutes and then transfer to a serving platter. Serve hot and enjoy.

241. Pepper Egg

(Time: 5 minutes \ Servings: 1)

Ingredients:

1 egg

1 large yellow bee pepper slice

1 pinch salt

1 pinch black pepper

2 tablespoons olive oil

Directions:

Spray the instant pot with oil. Place the bell pepper in the instant pot and crack the egg in the center.

Sprinkle salt and pepper. Cover with a lid and cook for 5 minutes on pressure cook mode.

Serve and enjoy.

242. Tomato Eggs

(Time: 10 minutes \ Servings: 2)

Ingredients:

2 eggs, whisked

2 tomatoes, sliced

1 teaspoon garlic powder

¼ teaspoons slat

½ teaspoon chili powder

3 tablespoons butter

Directions:

Melt butter on sauté mode. Add the eggs and spread all over. Cook for 1-2 minutes then flip.

Place the tomato slices and cover the pot with a lid, let it cook on pressure cooker mode for 10 minutes. Season with salt and chili powder. Serve hot and enjoy.

243. Instant Pot Zucchini Egg

(Time: 15 minutes \ Servings: 2)

Ingredients:

2 eggs, whisked

1 large zucchini, sliced

1 teaspoon garlic powder

¼ teaspoons slat

¼ teaspoon black pepper

3 tablespoons butter

Directions:

Melt butter in the instant pot on sauté mode. Fry zucchini for 3-4 minutes. Pour the eggs mixture and spread evenly.

Let it cook for 2-3 minutes from one side then flip it.

Season with salt and pepper.

Serve hot and enjoy.

244. Instant Pot Peperoni Pizza Egg

(Time: 15 minutes \ Servings: 2)

Ingredients:

2 eggs, whisked

1 teaspoon garlic powder

¼ teaspoons slat

½ teaspoon black pepper

1 onion, chopped

4-5 peperoni slices

3 tablespoons butter

Directions:

In eggs add onion, pepperoni, season with salt, garlic, and pepper. Melt butter in the instant pot on sauté mode. Pour the eggs mixture and spread all over.

Crumble with a fork and stir continuously. Cook for 1-2 minutes and then transfer to a serving platter. Serve hot and enjoy.

245. Instant Pot Egg Mac

(Time: 25 minutes \ Servings: 2)

Ingredients:

2 eggs, whisked

1 teaspoon garlic powder

¼ teaspoons slat

½ teaspoon black pepper

1 onion chopped

1 cup macaroni, boiled

1 tomato, chopped

3 tablespoons oil

Directions:

Combine the eggs with macaroni, onion, salt, pepper, and garlic powder, mix well. Heat oil in the instant pot on sauté mode. Pour the eggs mixture and spread all over.

Crumble with a fork by continuously stirring. Cook for 1-2 minutes and then transfer to a serving platter. Serve hot and enjoy.

246. Instant Pot Poached Eggs

(Time: 10 minutes \ Servings: 3)

Ingredients:

3 eggs

3 cups water

2 tablespoons vinegar

1 pinch salt

Directions:

Set the instant pot on pressure cook mode. Add water in the instant pot and let it boil.

Now crack 1 egg into a bowl and pour it in the boiled water. Repeat the step for all eggs. Cover with a lid and let it cook for 5 minutes. Ladle to a serving platter and enjoy.

247. Instant Pot Coated Eggs

(Time: 45 minutes \ Servings: 4)

Ingredients:

4 hardboiled eggs, peeled

1 teaspoon garlic powder

¼ teaspoons slat

½ teaspoon black pepper

1 cup chicken mince

2 tablespoons gram flour

1 cup oil, for frying

Directions:

Combine gram flour, mince, garlic powder, salt and pepper, mix well. Take 2-3 tablespoons of this mixture in hand and coat the egg in it. Repeat for all eggs.

Heat oil in the instant pot on sauté mode.

Fry eggs until nicely golden. Place to a paper towel.

Serve hot and enjoy.

248. Instant Pot Cabbage Egg

(Time: 15 minutes \ Servings: 2)

Ingredients:

2 eggs, whisked

1 teaspoon garlic powder

¼ teaspoons slat

½ teaspoon black pepper

½ cup parmesan cheese, shredded

1 cup cabbage, chopped

3 tablespoons butter

Directions:

In the whisked eggs, add cabbage, parmesan cheese, season with salt, garlic, and pepper. Melt butter in the instant pot on sauté mode. Pour the eggs mixture and spread evenly.

Cook for 2-3 minutes from one side then flip it. Cook for 1-2 minutes and then transfer to a serving platter. Serve hot.

249. Instant Pot Spinach Egg Frittata

(Time: 25 minutes \ Servings: 2)

Ingredients:

2 eggs, whisked

1 cup spinach, chopped

1 cup cherry tomatoes, sliced

¼ teaspoons slat

½ teaspoon black pepper

3 tablespoons butter

Directions:

In the whisked eggs, add spinach, tomatoes, season with salt, garlic, and pepper. Melt butter in the instant pot on sauté mode. Pour the eggs mixture and spread all over.

Let it cook for 2-3 minutes from one side then flip it.

Cook for 1-2 minutes and then transfer to a serving platter.

Serve hot and enjoy.

250. Ginger Zest Cauliflower Egg Soup

(Time: 25 minutes \ Servings: 3)

Ingredients:

1 cup cauliflower florets

1 teaspoon ginger paste

1 red bell pepper chopped

2 cups vegetable broth

2 tablespoons vinegar

1 lemon, sliced

2 eggs, whisked

1 green chili, chopped

4-5 garlic cloves, minced

½ teaspoon black pepper

¼ teaspoon salt

1 pinch turmeric powder

1 tablespoon oil

Directions:

Heat oil in the instant pot, add ginger paste and cook for 1 minute on sauté mode.

Add cauliflower and fry for 5-10 minutes.

Now add the bell pepper, salt, pepper, vinegar, turmeric powder, green chilies, lemon slices and mix well.

Add the vegetable broth and cook on medium heat for 15 minutes on stew mode.

Pour the eggs and stir continuously for 1 minute.

Ladle into a serving bowl.

Serve and enjoy

Instant Pot Fish Recipes

251. Lemon Fish Steaks

(Time: 25 minutes \ Servings: 3)

Ingredients:

4 fish fillets

2 tablespoons extra-virgin olive oil

1 teaspoon fine sea salt

1 teaspoon black pepper

Lemon wedges, for serving

2 tablespoons lemon juice

Directions:

Sprinkle salt and pepper on the fish. Drizzle lemon juice and oil, rub all over. Place it into a greased instant pot and cook for 15 minutes on pressure cooker mode. Serve with lemon wedges.

252. Curry Fish

(Time: 25 minutes \ Servings: 3)

Ingredients:

Fish fillet 4

½ tablespoon salt

½ tablespoon black pepper

2 tablespoons white vinegar

½ cup of tomato curry

½ tablespoon red paprika powder

1 clove of garlic, minced

1 onion, chopped

Bread crumbs as required

Oil for frying

Directions:

Take a large bowl, place the fish fillets and sprinkle salt, black pepper; roll in bread crumbs and place aside. Heat oil in the instant pot and fry the fish until golden. Cut into chunks and place aside.

In the instant pot, heat 2 tablespoons of oil on sauté mode.

Add another 1-2 tablespoons of oil, chopped onion, garlic and stir for 1-2 minutes. Add tomato puree, vinegar, salt, paprika, stir well and let it cook for 5-10 minutes on slow flame. Now put the fish chunks and add ½ cup of water or as much you like the consistency of the curry.

Cover with a lid and cook for 5-10 minutes on manual mode. Transfer to a dish and serve with boiled rice.

253. Creamy Tilapia

(Time: 25 minutes \ Servings: 3)

Ingredients:

½ lb. tilapia fillets

2 tablespoons lemon juice

2 tablespoons of lemon juice

½ teaspoon of black pepper

2 tablespoons chopped fresh dill weed

½ teaspoon salt

Cooking spray

Directions:

Grease the instant pot with a cooking spray and place the fish filets, sprinkle salt and dill.

Drizzle lemon juice and toss. Let it roast for 20 minutes on pressure cook mode.

After that, add cream cheese, black pepper and combine. Let it simmer for 2 minutes. Serve and enjoy.

254. Instant Pot Fried Fish

(Time: 25 minutes \ Servings: 4)

Ingredients:

4 fish fillets, cut into pieces

½ tablespoon salt

½ tablespoon black pepper

2 tablespoons white vinegar

½ tablespoon red paprika powder

1 teaspoon garlic paste

3 tablespoons gram flour

Oil for frying

Directions:

In a bowl, add all seasoning and mix well. Pour over the fish and rub all over. Now heat oil in the instant pot and fry the fish pieces until nicely golden. Serve and enjoy.

255. Instant Pot Fish Stew

(Time: 35 minutes \ Servings: 4)

Ingredients:

2 fish fillets, fried, cut into pieces

½ tablespoon salt

½ tablespoon chili power

1 teaspoon ginger garlic paste

2 tablespoons oil

1 cup tomato puree

2 green bell peppers, chopped

1 cup chicken broth

Directions:

Heat oil in the instant pot and fry the ginger garlic paste for 1 minutes. Add tomatoes and fry well.

Season with salt and chili powder. Now add the fried fish and bell pepper, toss well. Stir fry for 10 minutes. Pour in the chicken broth and cook on stew mode for 15 minutes. Serve and enjoy.

256. Instant Pot Roasted Fish with Vegetables

(Time: 25 minutes \ Servings: 4)

Ingredients:

2 tomatoes, sliced

1 avocado, chopped

1 onion, sliced

1 bunch green coriander, chopped

½ cup tomato puree

1 teaspoon garlic paste

Salt and black pepper to taste

2 fish fillets, cut into pieces

1 teaspoon lemon juice

Directions:

Heat oil in the instant pot and fry garlic and onion for 1 minutes. Add the fish and fry until nicely golden. Add tomatoes and keep frying. Season with salt and chili powder.

Now add avocado, tomato puree, and lemon juice, let it simmer for 10 minutes. Sprinkle coriander. Transfer to a serving platter and serve.

257. Instant Pot Creamy Tuna with Macaroni

(Time: 25 minutes \ Servings: 3)

Ingredients:

½ lb. tuna, cut into pieces

1 cup cream

1 teaspoon garlic paste

Salt and black pepper to taste

1 cup macaroni, boiled

Directions:

Heat oil in the instant pot and fry garlic for about 30 seconds. Add the fish and sauté it for 1-2 minutes. Season with salt and pepper. Stir in macaroni and cream, mix well. Transfer to a serving platter and serve.

258. Instant Pot Maple Zest Fish

(Time: 25 minutes \ Servings: 3)

Ingredients:

2 fish fillets

4 tablespoons maple syrup

2 garlic cloves, minced

Salt and black pepper to taste

2 tablespoons soya sauce

Directions:

Heat oil in the instant pot and fry garlic for 30 seconds. Add fish and sauté it for a minute or two.

Season with salt and pepper. Drizzle maple syrup and soya sauce. Toss well. Let it simmer for 5 minutes. Transfer to a serving platter and serve.

259. Instant Pot Fried Fish Fingers

(Time: 25 minutes \ Servings: 3)

Ingredients:

2 fish fillets, cut into 1inch strips

½ tablespoon salt

½ tablespoon black pepper

1 teaspoon garlic powder

3 tablespoons gram flour

1 teaspoon rosemary

Oil for frying

Directions:

In a bowl, add all seasoning and mix well. Add in the fish fingers and toss well. Now heat oil in the instant pot and fry the fish pieces until golden. Serve and enjoy.

260. Fried Tuna with Tamarind Sauce

(Time: 25 minutes \ Servings: 3)

Ingredients:

3 tuna fish fillets

2 tablespoons extra-virgin olive oil

1 teaspoon fine sea salt

1 teaspoon black pepper

Lemon wedges, for serving

2 tablespoons lemon juice

Directions:

Sprinkle salt and pepper on the fish. Then drizzle lemon juice and oil, rub all over the fish. Place it into a greased instant pot and cook for 15 minutes on pressure cooker. Serve with lemon wedges.

261. Instant Pot Fish Fry with Beans

(Time: 25 minutes \ Servings: 3)

Ingredients:

2 red bell peppers, chopped

1 teaspoon tarragon

1 cup green beans

1 teaspoon garlic paste

Salt and black pepper to taste

2 fish fillets, cut into pieces

1 teaspoon lemon juice

Directions:

Heat oil in the instant pot and fry garlic and onion for 1 minutes. Add the fish and fry well until golden brown. Season with salt and chili powder.Now add beans, bell pepper; simmer for 10 minutes.

Sprinkle tarragon and toss. Transfer to a serving platter and serve.

262. Instant Pot Crispy Crum Fish

(Time: 25 minutes \ Servings: 3)

Ingredients:

2 fish fillets

1 cup bread crumbs

1 egg, whisked

½ tablespoon salt

½ tablespoon black pepper

1 teaspoon garlic powder

Oil for frying

Directions:

In a bowl, add bread crumbs, salt, pepper, garlic and toss well. Dip the fish fillet in the egg and then roll out in the bread crumbs. Now heat oil in the instant pot and fry fish pieces until golden brown on sauté mode.

Serve and enjoy.

263. Instant Pot Fish Soul Satisfying Soup

(Time: 35 minutes \ Servings: 2)

Ingredients:

1 teaspoon saffron

1 teaspoon garlic paste

Salt and black pepper to taste

2 fish fillets, cut into pieces

1 cup cream

1 pinch chili powder

1 cup milk

Directions:

Heat oil in the instant pot and fry garlic with onion for 1 minutes. Add the fish and fry well until golden brown. Season with salt and chili powder. Now shred the fish with a fork and transfer again to the pot.

Add in the cream and milk, mix well. Simmer for 10 minutes on low heat. Sprinkle chili powder and saffron on top while serving.

264. Instant Pot Fish and Lettuce Salad

(Time: 25 minutes \ Servings: 3)

Ingredients:

2 fish fillets, cut into pieces

½ tablespoon salt

½ tablespoon black pepper

2 tablespoons white vinegar

1 cup lettuce leaves, sliced

1 teaspoon garlic powder

1 cup cream

Oil for frying

Directions:

Sprinkle salt, garlic, and pepper on the fish. In the instant pot, heat oil on sauté mode. Fry the fish until golden. Toss it with lettuce and add the cream.

Serve and enjoy.

265. Instant Pot Fish Patties

(Time: 35 minutes \ Servings: 3)

Ingredients:

2 fish fillets, cut into pieces

½ tablespoon salt

½ tablespoon black pepper

1 tablespoon coriander, chopped

¼ teaspoon garlic paste

4 tablespoons of gram flour

1 potato, boiled

½ cup oil for frying

Directions:

Heat 2 tablespoons of oil on sauté mode. Fry the fish until lightly golden. Now crumble with a fork and place aside. Combine the fish, potatoes, garlic, coriander, salt, and pepper and mix well.

Make small round patties with this mixture and place into a platter. Heat oil in the instant pot and shallow fry the patties on sauté mode until lightly golden. Serve with any sauce.

266. Instant Pot Fish with Tomatoes

(Time: 25 minutes \ Servings: 2)

Ingredients:

2 fish fillets, cut into pieces

½ tablespoon salt

½ tablespoon black pepper

¼ teaspoon garlic powder

2-3 tomatoes, sliced

2 tablespoons oil

Directions:

Heat oil on sauté mode. Fry the fish until lightly golden. Season with salt, pepper, garlic powder and add tomatoes.

Cover with a lid and cook on stew mode for 15 minutes.

Serve and enjoy.

267. Instant Pot Fish Mince with Marconi

(Time: 25 minutes \ Servings: 4)

Ingredients:

1 cup ground fish

½ tablespoon salt

½ tablespoon black pepper

¼ teaspoon garlic powder

1 cup peas, boiled

1 package macaroni

2 tablespoons oil

Directions:

Heat oil on sauté mode. Fry the ground fish until lightly golden with garlic powder, salt and pepper.

Add the peas and macaroni and cook for 5 minutes. Serve and enjoy.

268. Instant Pot Salmon Bowl

(Time: 15 minutes \ Servings: 2)

Ingredients:

2 salmon fillets, cut into pieces

½ tablespoon salt

½ tablespoon black pepper

¼ teaspoon garlic powder

1 cup lettuce leaves

1 tomato, chopped

2 tablespoons oil

Directions:

In the instant pot, heat oil on sauté mode. Stir fry the lettuce for 1 minute, place aside.

In the same pot, fry the fish until lightly golden. Season with salt, pepper and garlic powder.

Transfer to a serving platter and serve with lettuce and tomatoes.

Enjoy.

269. Instant Pot Fish Stew

(Time: 25 minutes \ Servings: 2)

Ingredients:

1 fish fillet, cut into small pieces

½ tablespoon salt

½ tablespoon black pepper

¼ teaspoon garlic powder

2 cups chicken broth

1 tablespoons green onion

2 tablespoons oil

Directions:

In the instant pot, add all ingredients and stir well. Let it cook on stew mode for 25 minutes. Serve hot and enjoy.

270. Instant Pot Tarragon Steamed Fish

(Time: 25 minutes \ Servings: 3)

Ingredients:

2 fish fillets, cut into pieces

½ tablespoon salt

½ tablespoon black pepper

2 tablespoons tarragon

¼ teaspoon garlic paste

2 tablespoons oil

Directions:

In the instant pot, place a rack and fill the pot with 2 cups water. Season the fish with salt, pepper, tarragon, garlic; rub well.

Place the fish on the rack and cover with a lid. Cook for 25 minutes until softened.

Serve and enjoy.

271. Instant Pot Whitebait Capers

(Time: 25 minutes \ Servings: 2)

Ingredients:

3 whitebait fillets

½ tablespoon salt

½ tablespoon black pepper

¼ teaspoon garlic paste

1 tablespoons capers

1 tablespoons sun dried tomatoes

2 tablespoons oil

2 tablespoons lime juice

Directions:

In the instant pot, add all ingredients and cook for 5 minutes on manual mode. Serve and enjoy.

272. Instant Pot Fish Tamarind Gravy

(Time: 45 minutes \ Servings: 3)

Ingredients:

3-4 fish fillets, pieces

½ tablespoon salt

½ tablespoon chili powder

¼ cup tamarind pulp

½ cup of tomato curry

1 clove of garlic, minced

1 onion, chopped

Oil for frying

Directions:

Take a large bowl and put the fish fillets inside. Sprinkle salt, black pepper and place into a platter.

Heat oil in the instant pot and fry fish until golden. Cut into chunks and place aside. Then heat 2 tablespoons of oil on sauté mode. Add 1-2 tablespoons of oil, chopped onion, garlic and stir for 1-2 minutes.

Add tomato puree, tamarind pulp, salt, paprika, stir well and let it cook for 5-10 minutes on slow flame. Now put the fish chunks and add ½ cup of water or as much you like for the consistency of the curry.

Cover with a lid and let it cook for 5-10 minutes on manual mode. Transfer to a dish and serve it with boiled rice.

273. Instant Pot Fish Smash

(Time: 35 minutes \ Servings: 3)

Ingredients:

½ tablespoon salt

3-4 tuna fillets

½ tablespoon black pepper

1 clove of garlic, minced

2 tablespoons oil

1 teaspoon basil, chopped

1 cup cream

Directions:

Heat oil on sauté mode. Add the fish and fry on low heat. Now put to a platter and scramble with a fork. Transfer to the pot again and add cream, salt, pepper, garlic and let it simmer for 2-3 minutes.

Serve and enjoy.

274. Instant Pot Coconut Fish

(Time: 45 minutes \ Servings: 3)

Ingredients:

3-4 fish fillets, pieces

½ tablespoon salt

½ tablespoon chili powder

½ cup coconut, crushed

1 cup coconut milk

1 clove of garlic, minced

Oil for frying

Directions:

Take a large bowl and put the fish fillets inside.

Then sprinkle salt, black pepper and place into a platter.

Heat oil in instant pot and fry the fish until golden.

Heat two tablespoons of oil on sauté mode.

Add garlic and fry for another minute.

Add fish, coconut, coconut milk and let it simmer on stew mode for 10 minutes.

Place to a dish and serve it with boiled rice.

275. Instant Pot Fish and Peas Salad

(Time: 45 minutes \ Servings: 3)

Ingredients:

3-4 fish fillets, pieces

½ tablespoon salt

½ tablespoon black pepper

1 cup cream

1 cup peas, boiled

1 clove of garlic, minced

2 tablespoons oil

Directions:

In instant pot, heat 2 tablespoons of oil on sauté mode.

Add garlic and fry for 1 minute.

Add the fish and stir fry for 5-10 minutes.

Transfer to a bowl and shred it well.

In a bowl combine the fish, peas, cream, and mix well.

Season with salt and pepper.

Transfer to a dish and serve it with boiled rice.

276. Instant Pot Mutton Pilaf

(Time: 45 minutes \ Servings: 5)

Ingredients:

2 cups rice, soaked

1 cup broccoli florets

3 oz. mutton, boiled, pieces

1 teaspoon cumin seeds

1 bay leaf

2 garlic cloves, minced

1 teaspoon black pepper

1 pinch turmeric powder

1 teaspoon cumin powder

2 tomatoes, chopped

2 medium onions, sliced

1 teaspoon salt

3 tablespoons olive oil

4 cups chicken broth

Directions:

Heat oil in the instant pot on sauté mode, fry onion with cumin seeds, and bay leaf until nicely golden. Add tomatoes and fry well. Now add the mutton and fry. Season with salt, turmeric powder, pepper, garlic and fry well.

Pour in vegetable broth and add cumin powder, cinnamon powder, let it boil. Add rice, let it simmer until baubles appear on surface, cover with a lid. Let it cook on medium heat for 20 minutes on rice mode. Transfer to a serving dish and enjoy.

277. Instant Pot Mutton Gravy

(Time: 60 minutes \ Servings: 4)

Ingredients:

4 oz. mutton, boiled

1 cup tomato puree

1 inch ginger slice

½ teaspoon garlic paste

1 teaspoon salt

¼ teaspoon chili powder

1 cup water

½ teaspoon cumin powder

4 tablespoons oil

Directions:

Heat oil in the instant pot on sauté mode and fry tomatoes with chili powder, ginger, garlic, and salt for 5-10 minute. Add mutton and fry well. Add in water and cook on stew mode for 15-20 minutes.

Sprinkle cumin powder and transfer to a serving dish. Enjoy.

278. Instant Pot Ground Beef Risotto

(Time: 25 minutes \ Servings: 3)

Ingredients:

1 cup ground beef

1 cup tomato ketchup

1 inch ginger slice, chopped

2 tablespoons brown sugar

1 teaspoon salt

¼ teaspoon chili powder

4 tablespoons oil

Directions:

Heat oil in the pot on sauté mode and fry the ground beef with ginger for 10 minutes. Add tomato ketchup, salt, chili powder, brown sugar and toss. Cook for 15-20 minutes. Serve with noodles and enjoy.

279. Slow Cooked Meat Tomato Chili

(Time: 120 minutes \ Servings: 3)

Ingredients:

2 oz. beef, pieces

¼ cup tomato ketchup

1 cup chili garlic sauce

1 teaspoon salt

1 cup white beans, soaked

½ cup tomato puree

3 cups chicken broth

2-3 garlic cloves

4 tablespoons oil

Directions:

In the instant pot, add all ingredients and cook for 120 minutes on slow cook mode. Serve and enjoy.

280. Ground Meat Lemonade

(Time: 40 minutes \ Servings: 3)

Ingredients:

2 cups beef mince

1 teaspoon salt

2 tablespoons lemon juice

¼ teaspoon chili powder

2 tomatoes, chopped

2-3 garlic cloves, minced

4 tablespoons oil

Directions:

Heat oil in the instant pot and fry garlic for 30 seconds.

Add the mince and fry well until its color changes. Season with salt and pepper.

Add tomatoes and stir fry for 10-15 minutes on high heat with a few splashes of water.

Drizzle lemon juice on top. Serve and enjoy.

281. Slow Cooked Meat Bruschetta

(Time: 120 minutes \ Servings: 3)

Ingredients:

2 oz. beef, pieces

1 cup tomato sauce

1 teaspoon salt

3 cups chicken broth

2-3 garlic cloves

4 tablespoons oil

Directions:

In the instant pot, add all ingredients and cook for 120 minutes on slow cook mode.

Serve and enjoy.

282. Carrot and Pork Stew

(Time: 45 minutes \ Servings: 7)

Ingredients:

1 onion, chopped

2 tomatoes, chopped

2 carrots, sliced

3 oz. pork meat, pieces, boiled

2 cups chicken broth

½ teaspoon garlic paste

½ teaspoon ginger paste

½ teaspoon cumin powder

½ teaspoon cinnamon power

½ teaspoon chili powder

¼ teaspoon salt

¼ teaspoon turmeric powder

3 tablespoons oil

2 green chilies, whole

Directions:

Heat oil in the instant pot, sauté onion for 1 minute on sauté mode. Stir in tomatoes, ginger garlic paste, salt, chili powder, turmeric powder and fry for 1 minute. Now add the pork, and fry for about 10 minutes. Add carrots and fry with them with the meat until lightly tendered.

Now add the chicken broth, green chili, and leave to cook on low heat for 30 minutes on stew mode. Add cinnamon and cumin powder and stir. Transfer to a serving dish and enjoy.

283. Instant Pot Spicy Pork Korma

(Time: 40 minutes \ Servings: 4)

Ingredients:

3 oz. pork, boiled

½ teaspoon garlic paste

1 teaspoon salt

2 tomatoes, chopped

½ teaspoon chili powder

¼ teaspoon turmeric powder

1 cup vegetable broth

½ teaspoon cumin powder

½ teaspoon dry coriander powder

3 tablespoons oil

Directions:

Heat oil on sauté mode and fry garlic for 1 minute. Add the tomatoes with salt, chili powder, turmeric powder and fry. Add in the pork pieces and stir fry with a few splashes of water until oil disappears from the sides of pan.Let it simmer on low heat for 10 minutes.

Pour in the vegetable broth and mix well. Cook on slow cook mode for 30 minutes. Season with cumin powder and dry coriander powder. Transfer to a serving dish and enjoy.

284. Instant Pot Beef Orzo

(Time: 40 minutes \ Servings: 4)

Ingredients:

1 cup orzo

¼ cup spinach, chopped

3 oz. beef, boiled

½ teaspoon garlic paste

1 teaspoon salt

2 tablespoons soya sauce

2 tomatoes, chopped

½ teaspoon chili powder

¼ teaspoon turmeric powder

2 cups vegetable broth

3 tablespoons oil

Directions:

In the instant pot, add all ingredients and cook on slow cook mode for 120 minutes. Serve and enjoy.

285. Instant Pot Hot Shredded Pork

(Time: 30 minutes \ Servings: 4)

Ingredients:

2 pork fillets, boiled, shredded

½ teaspoon garlic paste

½ teaspoon salt

½ teaspoon soya sauce

2 tablespoon lemon juice

2 tablespoons barbecue sauce

½ cup chili garlic sauce

2 tablespoons vinegar

½ teaspoon chili powder

2 tablespoons oil

Directions:

Heat oil on sauté mode and fry garlic for 1 minute. Place the pork and fry well. Add soya sauce, chili garlic sauce, vinegar, barbecue sauce, salt, chili powder and fry well. Transfer to a serving dish and drizzle lemon juice. Enjoy.

286. Instant Pot Mutton and Tomato Stew

(Time: 55 minutes \ Servings: 4)

Ingredients:

1 cup tomato puree	1 red chili
1 cup mutton, pieces, boiled	¼ teaspoon salt
2 tablespoons chili garlic sauce	¼ teaspoon black pepper
2 cups chicken broth	2 tablespoons cooking oil
1 garlic clove minced	

Directions:

In the instant pot, add tomato puree, mutton, chicken broth, salt, pepper, garlic, chili, chili garlic sauce, oil, and stir well. Cover with a lid and let it cook on stew mode for 40 minutes.

Transfer the soup to a blender and blend until puree. Transfer to the pot again and let it simmer for 5 minutes. Pour to a serving dish and enjoy.

287. Instant Pot Mushroom and Mutton Curry

(Time: 45 minutes \ Servings: 5)

Ingredients:

½ lb. mutton, boiled	¼ teaspoon cumin powder
1 cup mushrooms, sliced	¼ teaspoon cinnamon powder
1 onion, chopped	1 teaspoon salt
2-3 garlic cloves, minced	½ teaspoon chili powder
2 tomatoes, chopped	4 tablespoons olive oil
1 carrot, chopped	½ cup chicken broth
¼ teaspoon turmeric powder	1 green chili

Directions:

Heat oil in the instant pot and fry onion for 1 minute.

Add in the tomatoes, chili powder, salt, turmeric powder and fry.

Now add the mutton and stir fry well. Then add the carrot, mushrooms and stir fry for about 5-6 minutes.

Add the chicken broth in and cook on manual mode for 10-15 minutes. Sprinkle cumin powder and cinnamon powder, toss well. Transfer to a serving dish. Enjoy.

288. Instant Pot Fenugreek and Beef Curry

(Time: 55 minutes \ Servings: 5)

Ingredients:

½ lb. beef, boiled

½ cup fenugreek, chopped

1 onion, chopped

2-3 garlic cloves, minced

2 tomatoes, chopped

¼ teaspoon turmeric powder

¼ teaspoon cumin powder

¼ teaspoon cinnamon powder

1 teaspoon salt

½ teaspoon chili powder

4 tablespoons olive oil

½ cup chicken broth

1 green chili

Directions:

Heat oil in the instant pot on sauté mode and fry onion for 1 minute. Add in tomatoes, chili powder, salt, turmeric powder and fry. Then add the beef and stir fry for 5-10 minutes on high heat.

Now add the fenugreek and let it simmer for 5 minutes.

Add the chicken broth in and cook on manual mode for 10-15 minutes.

Sprinkle cumin powder and cinnamon powder, toss well. Transfer to a serving dish. Enjoy.

289. Instant Pot Pork Chops Gravy

(Time: 55 minutes \ Servings: 5)

Ingredients:

½ lb. pork chops

1 onion, chopped

2-3 garlic cloves, minced

2 tomatoes, chopped

¼ teaspoon turmeric powder

¼ teaspoon cumin powder

¼ teaspoon cinnamon powder

1 teaspoon salt

½ teaspoon chili powder

4 tablespoons olive oil

½ cup chicken broth

1 green chili

Directions:

Heat oil on sauté mode and fry onion for 1 minute. Add in the tomatoes, chili powder, salt, turmeric powder and fry. Now add the pork chops and stir fry for 5-10 minutes on high heat.

Add the chicken broth on and cook on manual mode for 10-15 minutes. Sprinkle cumin powder and cinnamon powder, toss well. Place to a serving dish and enjoy.

290. Slow Cooked Mutton Masala

(Time: 120 minutes \ Servings: 5)

Ingredients:

½ lb. mutton, boiled

1 onion, chopped

1 teaspoon ginger paste

½ teaspoon garlic paste

1 teaspoon salt

¼ teaspoon black pepper

3 tablespoons oil

Directions:

In the instant pot, add all ingredients and cook on slow cook mode for 2 hours. Stir occasionally.

Serve with boiled noodles and enjoy.

291. Instant Pot Mutton Broth

(Time: 60 minutes \ Servings: 4)

Ingredients:

½ lb. mutton, pieces

3-4 garlic cloves

1 teaspoon salt

¼ teaspoon black pepper

½ teaspoon chili powder

1 onion, sliced

1 inch ginger slice

5 cups water

¼ teaspoon turmeric powder

¼ teaspoon dry coriander powder

1 cinnamon stick

3 tablespoons oil

Directions:

In the instant pot, add all ingredients and cook on slow cook mode for 2 hours. Stir occasionally. Serve and enjoy.

292. Instant Pot Pork Steaks

(Time: 65 minutes \ Servings: 5)

Ingredients:

2 pork fillets

1 teaspoon garlic powder

½ teaspoon chili powder

2 tablespoons soya sauce

4 tablespoons barbecue sauce

¼ teaspoon turmeric powder

1 teaspoon salt

2 tablespoons vinegar

4 tablespoons olive oil

Directions:

In a bowl, add vinegar, soya sauce, barbecue sauce, chili powder, salt, garlic powder, and oil.

Transfer to the instant pot and cook on pressure cook mode for 60 minutes.

Serve and enjoy..

293. Instant Pot Mutton Peas

(Time: 55 minutes \ Servings: 4)

Ingredients:

½ lb. mutton, pieces, boiled

1 cup peas

1 onion, chopped

2-3 garlic cloves, minced

2 tomatoes, chopped

¼ teaspoon turmeric powder

¼ teaspoon cumin powder

¼ teaspoon cinnamon powder

1 teaspoon salt

½ teaspoon chili powder

4 tablespoons olive oil

½ cup chicken broth

1 green chili

Directions:

Heat oil on sauté mode and fry onion for 1 minute. Add in the tomatoes, chili powder, salt, turmeric powder and fry. Now add the mutton and stir fry for 5-10 minutes on high heat.

Stir in the peas and fry well. Add the chicken broth on and cook on manual mode for 10-15 minutes.

Sprinkle cumin powder and cinnamon powder, toss well. Serve and enjoy.

294. Instant Pot Pork Mutton Potato Curry

(Time: 55 minutes \ Servings: 5)

Ingredients:

½ lb. mutton, pieces, boiled

1 onion, chopped

2-3 potatoes, peeled, diced

2-3 garlic cloves, minced

2 tomatoes, chopped

¼ teaspoon turmeric powder

¼ teaspoon cumin powder

¼ teaspoon cinnamon powder

1 teaspoon salt

½ teaspoon chili powder

4 tablespoons olive oil

½ cup chicken broth

1 green chili

Directions:

Heat oil on sauté mode and fry onion for 1 minute. Add in the tomatoes, chili powder, salt, turmeric powder and fry. Now add the mutton and stir fry for 5-10 minutes on high heat.

Then add the potatoes and fry well. After that, add the chicken broth on and cook on manual mode for 10-15 minutes. Sprinkle cumin powder and cinnamon powder, toss well. Serve and enjoy.

295. Instant Pot Mutton and Yogurt

(Time: 55 minutes \ Servings: 5)

Ingredients:

½ lb. mutton, boiled

1 cup yogurt

1 onion, chopped

2-3 garlic cloves, minced

2 tomatoes, chopped

¼ teaspoon turmeric powder

¼ teaspoon cumin powder

¼ teaspoon cinnamon powder

1 teaspoon salt

½ teaspoon chili powder

4 tablespoons olive oil

½ cup chicken broth

1 green chili

Directions:

Heat oil in the instant pot on sauté mode and fry onion for 1 minute.

Add in the tomatoes, chili powder, salt, turmeric powder and fry. Now add the mutton pieces and stir fry for 5-10 minutes on high heat.

Stir in yogurt and fry until the oil disappears from the sides of the pan.

Then add the chicken broth on and let it cook on manual mode for 10-15 minutes. Sprinkle cumin powder and cinnamon powder, toss well.

Transfer to a serving dish and serve.

296. Instant Pot Beef Okra

(Time: 55 minutes \ Servings: 4)

Ingredients:

½ lb. mutton, boiled

1 cup okra

1 onion, chopped

2-3 garlic cloves, minced

2 tomatoes, chopped

¼ teaspoon turmeric powder

1 teaspoon salt

½ teaspoon chili powder

4 tablespoons olive oil

Directions:

Heat oil in the instant pot and fry the okra until crispy; place aside. In the same pot, fry onion for 1 minute. Add in the tomatoes, chili powder, salt, turmeric powder and fry.

Now add the mutton and stir fry for 5-10 minutes on high heat. Then add the okra and mix well. Transfer to a serving dish, serve and enjoy.

297. Instant Pot Fried Bitter Guard with Beef

(Time: 45 minutes \ Servings: 4)

Ingredients:

½ lb. mutton, boiled, small pieces

1 cup bitter guard

1 onion, chopped

2-3 garlic cloves, minced

2 tomatoes, chopped

¼ teaspoon turmeric powder

1 teaspoon salt

½ teaspoon chili powder

4 tablespoons olive oil

Directions:

Heat oil in the instant pot and fry the bitter guard until golden brown; place aside.

In the same pot fry onion for 1 minute.

Add in the tomatoes, chili powder, salt, turmeric powder and fry.

Now add the mutton and stir fry for 5-10 minutes on high heat. Add the fried bitter guard and mix well. Transfer to a serving dish and enjoy.

298. Instant Pot Mutton and Turnip Stew

(Time: 65 minutes \ Servings: 4)

Ingredients:

½ lb. mutton, boiled

3 turnips, peeled, diced

1 onion, chopped

2-3 garlic cloves, minced

2 tomatoes, chopped

¼ teaspoon turmeric powder

1 teaspoon salt

½ teaspoon chili powder

4 tablespoons olive oil

Directions:

In the instant pot, add all ingredients and toss. Let it cook for 60 minutes on slow cook mode.

Serve hot and enjoy.

299. Instant Pot Beef and Pumpkin

(Time: 65 minutes \ Servings: 4)

Ingredients:

½ lb. mutton, boiled

3 turnips, peeled, diced

1 onion, sliced

2-3 garlic cloves, minced

1 teaspoon salt

½ teaspoon chili powder

4 tablespoons olive oil

Directions:

In the instant pot, add all ingredients and toss. Let it cook for 60 minutes on slow cook mode.

Serve hot and enjoy.

300. Slow Cooked Zucchini and Pork

(Time: 65 minutes \ Servings: 5)

Ingredients:

½ lb. pork, pieces

2 zucchini, sliced

3 turnips, peeled, diced

1 onion, chopped

2-3 garlic cloves, minced

2 tomatoes, chopped

¼ teaspoon turmeric powder

1 teaspoon salt

½ teaspoon chili powder

4 tablespoons olive oil

Directions:

In the instant pot, add all ingredients and toss.

Let it cook for 60 minutes on slow cook mode.

Serve hot and enjoy.

DOWNLOAD THE PDF WITH IMAGES HERE:

goo.gl/oQFO5Q